THE HEALING AND PEACE OF FORGIVENESS

By

Dr. Samuel Walston, Jr.

Copyright © 2012 by Dr. Samuel Walston, Jr.

The Healing and Peace of Forgiveness
by Dr. Samuel Walston, Jr.

Printed in the United States of America

ISBN 9781622304998

All rights reserved solely by the author. The author guarantees all contents are original and do not infringe upon the legal rights of any other person or work. No part of this book may be reproduced in any form without the permission of the author. The views expressed in this book are not necessarily those of the publisher.

Unless otherwise indicated, Bible quotations are taken from the King James Version of the Bible.

TXU996-040

www.xulonpress.com

Contents

Foreword by William Hoffman		vii
Introduction		ix
	God Enters the Picture	xxvi
	Where Is Love	xxx
Chapter I	Corrupt Communication Destroys Desire to Forgive	39
Chapter II	Forgive and Forget	53
Chapter III	One of the Devil's Greatest Lies	57
Chapter IV	The Sore That Must Be Healed	63
Chapter V	Effect and Healing of Broken Relationships	70
Chapter VI	Physical Effects of Un-Forgiveness	83
Chapter VII	Cleansing and Healing Power of Jesus' Blood	92
	Atonement by the Blood of Animals	98
	Our Reconciliation	103
	Forgive Yourself	111
	Forgive Others	114
Chapter VIII	Housecleaning	121
	Broken Relationships	127
	Self Control	132
Chapter IX	Demolishing Demonic Walls of Un-Forgiveness	137

The Healing and Peace of Forgiveness

Chapter X	God's Provision for Forgiveness	145
	God's New Provision	156
	The Blessings for Forgiveness	160
	The Curses of Un-Forgiveness	163

Closing Statement by Barbara E. Walston 167

FOREWORD

By
William Hoffman

*A*ssume for the sake of argument that religion has nothing to say one way or the other on the question of forgiveness. If that were the case, the evidence would still be utterly compelling, even overwhelming, that we need to put past hurts, no matter how grievous, behind us. The power of forgiveness will not only strike a powerful chord among America's large religious community, but a wider general audience as well.

Un-forgiveness is unhealthy. If un-forgiveness were a product, it would be labeled hazardous to the user. It can cause anger, anxiety, depression — a wide variety of psychosomatic disorders that can trigger serious, even fatal, physical ailments and illnesses; increased blood sugar and blood pressure levels, sleep disorders, eating disorders, respiratory problems, and cardiovascular disease. These health disturbances and many others can be induced and aggravated by the stress and bitterness engendered by un-forgiveness.

Un-forgiveness is self – defeating. It can be compared to a petulant child saying, "I'll get even with you by hurting myself." As a matter of fact, un – forgiveness injures not

The Healing and Peace of Forgiveness

the person at whom it's aimed, but the individual doing the aiming. Holding on to grievances can consume a person in hatred, even in his last moments. Un – forgiveness prevents us from living healthy, productive, satisfying lives. It means that pain from the past is allowed to cause pain in the present. Absurd is seems, un – forgiveness is the same as saying, "I think I'll nurse this wound for the rest of my life and let it use up my energy and take away my peace of mind.

INTRODUCTION

(MY PERSONAL EXPERIENCE WITH BITTERNESS AND FORGIVENESS)

Amos 3:3 — shall two walk together, except they have agreed? (ASV)

In 1966 while I served a tour of duty with the United States Army in Germany, my wife Barbara became associated with the World Wide Church of God founded by Herbert W. Armstrong. We weren't attending church at the time and I really didn't concern myself with it. Because of what I had witnessed of church folk and had seen pastors do outside of church, I preferred not to join. Barbara, on the other hand, having grown up in church, recognized that we needed spiritual help.

As I went about my daily tasks, trying to earn another promotion, Barbara attended Bible Study conducted by the post chaplain, finding more questions than answers. Her first question: why was no Bible available at the Bible Study?

This represented a crucial time in my life because of the Vietnam War. One day Barbara shared some literature with me from the World Wide Church of God. After a few months of corresponding with the church, we got a telephone call from one of their ministers and arranged a meeting in Frankfurt. Although I enjoyed the conversation, I didn't know the difference between religion (a belief system) and Christianity (dedication to Christ). However, Barbara seemed pleased that I had gone with her to the meeting. I didn't share with her the bad experience I'd had with ministers in Korea.

Prior to my assignment in Germany, while stationed in Korea, I went to the post chaplain to inquire about becoming a church member.

"Why?" He asked.

What a dumb question, I thought. "Because, I need God." I had concluded that church membership would provide an avenue to God Who would take care of my family while I served in Korea.

When the chaplain turned me over to his assistant for further indoctrination, I didn't realize I had just met two messengers of Satan bent on driving men into the arms of Hell, hypocrites placed by the military into positions of Godly men.

My ears opened, awaiting spiritual revelations from these presumed representatives of God. Instead, my jaw dropped when the assistant casually mentioned his reason for going into the seminary: "To lure the faithful into my bed."

Not only were they not helpful but, as I listened to them discuss their lust for women, I knew my search for spiritual guidance from any military chaplain was over. This experience adversely affected me for the next five years. Consequently, when my wife and I met with the two ministers in Germany, I had a closed mind.

Matthew 7:15 Beware of false prophets, which come to you in sheep's clothing, but inwardly they are ravening wolves. (KJV)

Introduction

Upon completing my tour of duty in Germany, we returned to the states and later met with two more ministers from the World Wide Church of God in Fort Lee, Virginia. They visited our home about four times before we attended the church. I was impressed with their knowledge of the Bible. Unlike those men in Korea, these ministers quoted Scripture and knew the Bible. In the summer of 1968, my wife and I accepter Jesus Christ as our Savior and became members of the church.

During the next six years I received an intense teaching of the Old Testament: obey the Law of Moses, keep the Sabbath holy, tithe, observe feast days, the husband being head of the family, etc. I studied the Ambassador College Bible Correspondence Course and pored over all church literature.

In 1974, after attending the World Wide Church of God for approximately six years, we were asked to leave because I questioned some of the church doctrines. Since it was considered the "only true church of God," doubts about some of the doctrines were not welcomed by the leadership.

We went into that church seeking God and wholeheartedly believed the teachings. Later we learned that some were biblically based in error — a misunderstanding of Scriptures which led us to believe the World Wide Church of God was the "only true church of God." Therefore, over a period of time, we were indoctrinated to believe it. To be honest, I really didn't care if they were or not. I simply wanted to learn how to please God.

Acceptance of an only truth places you in a position where you cannot be ministered to by anyone outside of that sphere. In addition, as new members, we were warned not to question or engage in negative discussions of church doctrine. Such behavior could result in excommunication, ultimately separation from God for being put out of His only true church.

One of our local pastors had taught us to pray like Daniel, three times a day. Taking his teachings to heart, I prayed three hours daily and studied my Bible at least two hours daily. This positioned me to receive the Spirit of God's revelations from the Bible and help discerning truth from error.

I learned "church" meant "called out ones," which included anyone who accepted Jesus Christ as their Lord and Savior. To add to my newfound knowledge, I learned Jesus Christ was the head of the Church, and I need not fear any man removing me from the "only true church of God."

After service one Saturday, I asked our Senior Pastor a question about one of the church doctrines and showed him what the Bible stated. There were some inconsistencies. His answer: "The church teachings are right, regardless of what the Bible says." I could see the blood in his eyes and wondered how long he would let me stay in the church with my attitude.

Everything went fine until I wrote a paper including a statement that Herbert W. Armstrong was not similar to Moses, a mediator between God and man. That proved to be the last straw. The church leadership admonished us to conduct biblical research on the church doctrine and submit the report to the local pastor for mailing to church headquarters. Some of the leaders had taken it upon themselves to question doctrine they saw as biblically incorrect.

Mr. Armstrong traveled a great deal in those days, visiting various areas of the world. But getting wind of our actions, he cut a trip short. Herbert W. Armstrong considered anyone who questioned his doctrine as a heretic and accused them of trying to usurp their power over his divine authority. These men were removed immediately. Within days each member received a thirty page letter by mail explaining the details of the situation. I saw the handwriting on the wall.

The district pastor reviewed my report and had the local pastor set up a meeting with me. The local pastor insinuated

Introduction

that I could repent and stay in the church, as he had done. I knew in my heart God wanted me out of this church. Therefore, I had peace and stood on His Word. Their main concern about the report involved the damaging statement: "Mr. Armstrong doesn't have a divine position similar to that of Moses over all of God's people, and the World Wide Church of God is not the only true church of God." I must say the meeting was friendly but intense. Anyone could predict the conclusion: they excommunicated me, although they didn't disagree with any of the biblical answers I gave. The local pastor, who said little during the meeting, stayed with the church and became a director.

I then began studying the Bible at home alone for approximately two years looking for the truth. My goal: to find the difference between what they taught and what agreed with the Bible. I wanted to make sure I didn't view biblical truths based upon my past knowledge and experiences. I strove to see what the Bible said, not to prove or disprove what I had been taught.

Through prayer and Scripture study I learned two very important things: we will always be looking for biblical truths, and because of our imperfection, we will never know total truth until Jesus returns. The amount of knowledge we gain during our lives will depend on the time we put into obtaining it.

Isaiah 28:9-11 Whom shall he teach knowledge? and whom shall he make to understand doctrine? them that are weaned from the milk, and drawn from the breasts. For precept must be upon precept, precept upon precept; line upon line, line upon line; here a little, and there a little: For with stammering lips and another tongue will he speak to this people. (KJV)

The Healing and Peace of Forgiveness

As individuals, we each have our own unique way of responding to pressure and change. I became depressed a few months after leaving the World Wide Church of God. I came to realize that the foundation on which I so boldly stood had been destroyed. If the World Wide Church of God — as it so boldly proclaimed — was not the "only true church of God," then perhaps I could have actually been part of a cult.

My depression came from not understanding my spiritual condition, the loss of friends, and now growing spiritual problems within my family. I didn't understand the adverse effect stress could have on a person until I studied the subject some years later. The information listed below will give you some idea of what a person can experience.

Dr. Thomas H. Holmes and Dr. Reji of the University of Washington Medical School created a scale for measuring stress on a point system. Below is a table of stress areas I experienced:

STRESS SITUATIONS	POINTS
Personal Readjustment	39
Family Discussions	35
Heavier Responsibilities	29
Change of Personal Habits	24
Change of Church	19
Change of Social Activities	18
Total	164

(published by INTERPACIFIC Press, Health in the 21st Century; by Francisco Contreras MD. February 1997, page 318)

Holmes and his collaborators predicted illnesses using this scale. Almost half (49%) of people who accumulated

Introduction

300 points in a 12 – month period developed a critical illness, while only 9% of those accumulating less than 200 points in the same period fell ill. Arnold Huchnaker wrote, "Depression is a partial surrender to death and it seems that cancer is desperation at the cellular level." My stress factor, less than 200 points, could cause depression and other psychological problems. Stress elements from everyday pressures produce additional points not included.

Barbara took our children to a nondenominational church in Newport News, Virginia. I had a problem with this because I could not monitor what they were taught. I would have been destroyed if Barbara had taken our family into a church similar to the one we came from. Being separated from church and friends is considered severe. Most people rush to cover the hurt or disappointment by getting involved in something else as soon as possible. Divorced people do the same thing. They rush to another person and many times get married within months, only to end up with another divorce. My desires, as are the desires of most Godly husbands, were to protect my family. I believed then, as well as today, that the welfare and protection of my family are my responsibility.

I visited a few churches with Barbara but none of them taught the revelation I was learning, so I continued studying at home alone. Those were frustrating times, especially for Barbara who wanted me in church with her. But I'd become comfortable studying and waiting for God to show me what to do next. Thus, she asked her new congregation to pray for me. By this time, I had developed an intolerance for incorrect Bible teachings and used my wife as a sounding board for continually bashing ministers. I analyzed every church and their teachings very carefully. No matter what I tried to do for my family, my actions became repulsive.

We fail to understand this one fact: people can be depressed and suicidal while appearing normal. We are good actors. We must talk to families and friends, let them know we care about them, and offer help with their problems. Barbara and I both had problems. We were depressed and could not reach out to each other because we were trying to prove our points. During those years, we had actually separated ourselves from our family. We visited them but they couldn't reach us doctrinally. God's blessings saw us through a dangerous position and helped us to recover.

One night, while watching a Christian television program, I heard a minister teaching biblical principles I'd learned. This was my breakthrough. We hadn't listened to any ministers on television or radio while in the World Wide Church of God. The church emphasized the importance of their teachings and explained that the outside world couldn't understand them. I had been programmed to reject all information unlike what I had been taught. This is called mind control. It poisons the mind.

One Saturday in 1978, Barbara came home from a Ladies Prayer Breakfast and handed me her notes from the lecture. The pastor's wife presiding over the meeting taught some of the same things I had been learning. The next Wednesday night I took my family to that particular church's Bible study. I liked what I heard, and told Barbara I wanted the family to attend this church. A few months later Barbara informed me she was returning to her previous church. To my disappointment, she did not accompany me any more. Our problems began to snowball from that day to years later. I felt she had rebelled and usurped her authority over me, the head of the family. Such actions could destroy a weak father and a family, but I held my position with the children.

After approximately a year, I consulted my pastor but found he lacked the wisdom to help me cope with the situation. He stated I was right and she should attend church with me. In contrast, I later learned his wife had left him until he allowed her to control part of the ministry. His advice didn't help solve my problem.

During the following years my pastor informed me of upcoming promotions within the church, but because my wife was not a member, I didn't qualify. At first it didn't bother me, because I wasn't going to church to obtain a position. I went to that church because of the teaching I needed to complete what I was learning. My pastor taught a lot about the need for family togetherness, and husbands being the head of the family. As a matter of fact, most ministers were teaching similar messages. Hearing the same thing from several sources, I felt it was my responsibility to align my wife with the Word of God. Barbara disagreed and continued going to the other church.

I would look at my wife and get mad, thinking she prevented me from being promoted. The devil established a stronghold in my mind and worked his game of hatred. It took me years to understand that everything must be measured by the Word of God, not the words of man. Satan tries to use us to destroy each other's effectiveness in the ministry. One of the worst spirits in the Kingdom of Satan is the religious spirit. That evil spirit convinces each person involved that they are following the Word of God and the other person is trying to destroy their relationship with God.

This began to affect me negatively, and I truly thought Barbara kept me from serving God effectively because she did not worship with me. Looking back on my case and other events, I actually suspect some pastors purposely teach some areas of Scripture incorrectly to benefit themselves and their church. This is another reason why we must study God's Word for ourselves. God holds each of us responsible for obeying His Word. It took me years to understand the biblical view. Yes, it is God's will for families to worship together.

The Healing and Peace of Forgiveness

1 Timothy 3:1 This is a true saying, If a man desire the office of a bishop, he desireth a good work. A bishop then must be blameless, the husband of one wife, vigilant, sober, of good behaviour, given to hospitality, apt to teach; Not given to wine, no striker, not greedy of filthy lucre; but patient, not a brawler, not covetous; <u>One that ruleth well his own house, having his children in subjection with all gravity;</u> (For if a man knows not how to rule his own house, how shall he take care of the church of God?) Not a novice, lest being lifted up with pride he fall into the condemnation of the devil. Moreover he must have a good report of them which are without; lest he fall into reproach and the snare of the devil. Likewise must the deacons be grave, not doubletongued, not given to much wine, not greedy of filthy lucre; Holding the mystery of the faith in a pure conscience.
And let these also first be proved; then let them use the office of a deacon, being found blameless. Even so must their wives be grave, not slanderers, sober, faithful in all things. (KJV)

I believe a family can become stronger and draw closer by worshiping together. Unfortunately, it's not taught in all churches. The reason some pastors don't teach that a wife should worship with her husband is because many of their members would leave. Most churches have a larger population of women than men. When absentee husbands decide to attend or join another church, the wife's pastor may lose her as a member. Therefore, most pastors omit teaching this principle.

When I taught the truth on this issue some wives got mad because they weren't accustomed to hearing the truth.

One example: I had been a pastor for approximately six months when this lady came with her child. She informed me that God had given her a gift to minister to children. Good, we needed such a person. A few weeks later I learned she was married and her husband had a drug rehabilitation

Introduction

ministry in one of the local churches. When I asked why she wasn't attending there, she said the pastor didn't teach the Word. (This is a statement indicating the pastor may not be a "faith" teacher.) Knowing what the Lord required of me, I informed her she should be there to support her husband. She could minister to the children in that church and visit other churches. Don't get me wrong, but there is nothing stated in the Bible about making a married couple support one another. Only love has that power.

I heard Billy Graham say his wife was not of his denomination and had some different beliefs. If he had heard the teaching I did, he would have stayed home and millions would not have heard the salvation message. Many of the men and women of the Bible performed great exploits without their mates. In most cases, the mates aren't even mentioned, such as the wives of Peter, John, Paul, Stephen, Silas and Barnabas. Ideally speaking, of course, it is best for the husband and wife to work together. When they do, the results speak for themselves. God honoring the unity of husband and wife is depicted throughout the Bible.

Matthew 18:19-20 Again I say unto you, That if two of you shall agree on earth as touching any thing that they shall ask, it shall be done for them of my Father which is in heaven. For where two or three are gathered together in my name, there am I in the midst of them. (KJV)

After eight years of worshiping and serving in that particular church, I told the pastor I believed God was leading me to establish a ministry outside of the church. We met a couple of times and he offered me a job with the church. After praying and fasting, I informed him I could not accept his offer. We parted as always with a handshake and a hug. A few days later, I received a call from the assistant pastor stating he and the pastor decided I should find another

The Healing and Peace of Forgiveness

church. I couldn't believe it. What had I done? Is this the way to treat a person wanting to expand the ministry? Any ministry I established would have been a part of his church. Initially, I hadn't planned to leave the church. I was getting a lesson in religion and I learned fast to trust God only.

I made an appointment with the pastor and he agreed to ordain and commission me during a Wednesday night service. During that service he said I was "the most faithful man in the church." I knew the Holy Spirit spoke through him because if he really believed what he said his actions would have been different. I thought if this is the way you treat the most faithful man in your church, may God help the others.

My wife and I met with friends to talk and pray for clarity and direction because I felt the Spirit of the Lord directing me to start a church. While praying, God gave me a vision of my ministry. The magnitude of it overwhelmed me and I began to sob. What I saw in the spiritual realm was greater than I could handle. I didn't understand God's method at that time. He calls, then He prepares, and then He sends you out.

Some days later, while returning home from North Carolina, God gave me a name for the ministry: Eagle Life Ministries. After studying the life of the eagle, I saw the magnitude of what my calling required.

Establishing the church escalated my problems with Barbara, who simply didn't want to be a pastor's wife. She attended Eagle Life Ministries Church, and as soon as the service ended she left for the other church. Having women who wanted to talk to her about their problems, I asked her to stay for a while afterwards to counsel them. I preached to her how she should help me and, eventually, she stopped coming to our church. Although she continued tithing to Eagle Life Ministries, I wanted and needed her total support. Still, she insisted on attending elsewhere.

We had people coming to church who lived in unbelievably horrible conditions: families crowded into one room,

Introduction

broken homes, drug addiction. They were hurting and I was hurting. My hurt drove me to God and the Bible which enabled me to minister to them with all my heart. I cried for them and spent many hours praying for their freedom. I knew each message had to be anointed and powerful enough to set them free. I couldn't play pastor. Every day I took the battlefield in my home, in their homes, and in the church. God blessed us to see many of those people set free.

Barbara couldn't empathize with my desire to free people from misery. In addition, most mates don't understand that they are needed to satisfy each other's ego. During courtship we flatter and compliment, but after years of marriage, we tend to forget those small things that helped us through hard times. Please, don't leave this gap in your marriage. A wise person can see where they are falling short and move in to fill that gap. It happened that the Word of God took up my time. But prayer, daily Bible study and fasting once a week did not stop bitterness from developing. Nor did it stop women from coming out of the woodwork to tell me how much they appreciated my ministry.

I was told that a pastor, who I considered my friend, stated, "Why should anyone go to his church when his own wife won't go?" I didn't understand it then, but God must have given me a powerful ministry, because so many people were led by the devil to attack me.

Years before I started the church, God had led me to pray daily for those same pastors. I couldn't imagine a fellow pastor not wishing a colleague success in establishing a church for the Lord. I fought negative spiritual forces that tried to take over my entire life, but knew God had blessed me, my members, and my radio programs, although I felt plagued by a seemingly unmovable mountain.

I lapsed into bitterness. Whenever I saw my wife, I got mad. How could she support another minister and not me? I had provided for her and loved her since we were married at age 18. She never had to work away from the home or be concerned about the bills.

I spent countless hours studying the Bible, fasting, and praying for God to move her. What I considered a life or death situation affected my spirit and soul. I may actually have entered into hate. At times when I prayed, I thought of God removing her from the earth. Then, I had to repent and pray for forgiveness.

I considered divorce. I'd read about a congregation accepting its leader's divorce and marriage to a second wife. But this was not my answer. During prayer one day, the Lord through the Holy Spirit voiced displeasure with my line of thinking. The way I heard the Spirit speak: "Who told you to consider divorcing your wife?"

I quickly abandoned the idea.

Still, God continued to bless my ministry. So many times when I counseled others, I saw their problems clearly and wondered why they couldn't see the solution I provided them. Now, the same thing had happened to me. My wife and I enjoyed a wonderful relationship, except in this one area.

The solution didn't involve removing my wife from my life, nor the ministers who spoke against me. I needed to eliminate the devil and flesh from my life and move on with the work of the ministry. Easily said, but how could I scale this mountain? I had to learn to operate in true love. Every minister believes they walk in love; I did. But truth be told, I walked in "like." Not love.

It's easy to love and forgive those who follow us and do what we request. Discord arises when someone bucks us and thwarts our desires. I could not separate the ministry from my family life. You must understand something here. The day my wife decided to stop coming to our church an evil spiritual force began operating in our lives.

Introduction

It is hard to live with a person and not take their negative action as an affront. I took Barbara's personally. She had rejected me and chose to help someone else accomplish their God given call over her own husband's. I responded to her bitterly. Many readers have had similar experiences. How do we recover from this type of situation? With God's help, He uses whatever it takes to minister to our needs.

Through my prayers and days of fasting, God taught me to rely on Him. People sometimes become vindictive and bitterness turns to hate. Hatred can cause a person to kill. One day as Barbara and I returned from a walk by the water, I heard the word "death." I knew what it meant but didn't like it. Perhaps you've heard people on the news say after committing a violent crime that something told them to do it. Well, I heard the devil speaking. The devil will speak to you once you enter his territory, an area such as bitterness and hatred. At that moment, I realized I had to change my method of prayer and my attitude toward my wife in this area. It took time, but change did come. I began praying for God to lead my family into whichever ministry He could best use them.

When I allowed my mind to line up with the Word of God, I began seeing clearer. Why do we accept Christ and want everyone around us to change their desires just to please our commitments? During my time of praying and fasting, the Spirit of God asked if I wanted my children to obey me because I made them or because they loved me. You know the answer: love. I learned that love had to be the motivating factor behind all my actions. Love had to govern my life, regardless of what others did or didn't do.

I had to be healed of bitterness and hatred permanently, not whitewashed. Too often we hide our feelings until we explode with anger. During that period in my life I operated a ministry, worked a full – time job, had a radio ministry, spoke in various churches, and counseled people — all while waiting for the healing I so badly needed.

Unresolved difficulties with your mate have an awful way of spilling over to your children. I love my children and wife, but during those years it became hard to love anyone. I had to fight bad feelings every time I saw Barbara. I know thousands of families experience similar situations daily and, sadly, children are caught in the middle. You love them but the hatred and bitterness threatens to capture your entire being. Things like this going on turn a house cold not warm like a home should be with the love of God flowing through it.

The three – day fasting and prayer weekends I had each month helped save me. I'd reached a place where I did not want to live. My love for God and commitment to His Word kept me from destroying my own life. The devil will take a small incident and turn it into a mountain. Why was it so important to have a church? Why would God ask me to do something that would destroy my family? He wouldn't. But did He inform me to start a church? I believe He did. We have our spirit, mind and intuition which God may use to direct us. There are many examples I can share with you explaining how He directs me but I think this one is best:

> I was returning home from Durham, N.C., one Sunday afternoon some years ago. Normally I stopped at a particular hotel and ate. This time I decided not to, but the closer I got, my desire became stronger. So, I decided to stop and change my clothes in the restroom. As I turned into the parking lot, an elderly Caucasian woman standing outside her hotel room door fastened her eyes on my car and followed it into an available parking space near her. I got out of the car, went into the trunk for my clothes and walked around to the sidewalk. As I was about to speak, the lady looked at me with a frown and

said, "my head is hurting. It has been all day." I asked her if she knew Jesus Christ as her Savior. She did. I prayed for her and she went to her room, as I was while returning to my car after changing clothes, the lady came outside, and her pain was gone and she thanked me. God had a mission, I was in that area, and so He got my attention in a language I could understand: go change your clothes.

During the first four years of Eagle Life Ministries, a number of people accepted Jesus Christ as their Savior, and many were set free of their burdens. But the most impressive service occurred the Sunday that twelve children from the Special Olympic team attended. I established a rapport with a few of them before service. One young Afro- American came up to ask me about our recording machines. The chaperon instructed him to take his seat but I said it was all right. Suddenly, most of the other children came up to see the equipment and talk with me. Children know when you genuinely care about them. During my message they were on the edge of their seats. When I asked if anyone wanted to accept Christ as their Lord and Savior, they all came forward, plus two of the three chaperons. We had completed our mission.

God uses us to complete His mission. Peter ministered to the Jews, and Paul to the Gentiles. From 1903 to 1906, God used William J. Seymour, the Apostle of Azusa Street, a one – eyed Afro – American, in the greatest Holy Spirit renewal the world had ever seen. This renewal lasted three years, night and day, and at the end of his life this great man of God considered himself a failure. We must learn and understand God's methods.

When our children were young, we instructed them to hold a glass of water with both hands. As they grew older, the instructions changed. I learned that God looks for people to perform special jobs but it is hard to find those who can understand when the job is completed. Most of us look for assignments that will bring great returns. God looks for someone obedient to the leading of the Spirit.

1 Corinthians 12:3-12 Wherefore I give you to understand, that no man speaking by the Spirit of God calleth Jesus accursed: and that no man can say that Jesus is the Lord, but by the Holy Ghost. Now there are diversities of gifts, but the same Spirit. And there are differences of administrations, but the same Lord. And there are diversities of operations, but it is the same God which worketh all in all. But the manifestation of the Spirit is given to every man to profit withal. For to one is given by the Spirit the word of wisdom; to another the word of knowledge by the same Spirit; To another faith by the same Spirit; to another the gifts of healing by the same Spirit; To another the working of miracles; to another prophecy; to another discerning of spirits; to another divers kinds of tongues; to another the interpretation of tongues: But all these worketh that one and the selfsame Spirit, dividing to every man severally as he will. For as the body is one, and hath many members, and all the members of that one body, being many, are one body: so also is Christ. (KJV)

    God [ENTERS THE PICTURE] — In January of 1991, while attending a three – day ministerial conference in Durham, North Carolina, God manifested Himself to me by the Holy Spirit. I awakened about 4:30 a.m. knowing He had summoned me to pray. During that time in my life, I routinely arose early to pray and study my Bible before leaving home for work. Yet during the conference, I had planned to sleep late, until approximately 8 a.m., knowing I would still have time to pray before the first meeting. But I was surprised to have awakened so easily. I shuffled over to the window, opened the curtain slightly to allow in light from the security lamps outside and began praying.

Introduction

About thirty minutes into my prayers I felt as if the room had been transformed into a place of love and peace. The presence of the Lord had entered, changing the entire atmosphere. I could feel His presence but could not see Him with my natural eyes. I'd had similar experiences in the past and each time proved as awesome as the first.

Someone asked once how I knew the Spirit of the Lord from that of the devil. Well, I have also been in the presence of sinister spirits and know the difference between the two. Evil spirits make the atmosphere feel evil and cold, bringing an eerie uncomfortable sense of fear. They desire to destroy your life by using fear, or to possess your body and control your mind. The Spirit of God emanates love and comfort; the Spirit of Satan engenders fear.

The Spirit of the Lord and I began having a spiritual exchange. If you understand how a radio picks up sound waves, you'll understand how we talked spiritually. Different sound waves exist in the atmosphere. The amplitude modulation (AM), frequency modulation (FM), and short waves (SW) are all bands of radio – wave frequencies. We don't see them but we can pick them up by use of the proper radio and antenna. Spiritual waves can be picked up by the spirits of a people who have accepted Jesus Christ as their Savior and are walking in what they know is the path of the Word of God.

Some lawbreakers say, "I was told to do it." We who understand spiritual things know this is possible. Evil spirits will possess individuals and use them to commit crimes. The children who killed their parents were not evil themselves but directed by evil spirits. Their involvement in demonic books, music, television, radio programs, etc., allows devils to enter and rule their minds.

I could hear with my spiritual ears what the Spirit of the Lord was saying and could answer Him through my thoughts. The Holy Spirit is the representative of God in us and He enables us to talk directly to God. This way evil spirits cannot interfere with God's response to our prayers, nor can they know what is happening in the Spirit realm between us and the Father God. They can only discern events based on our actions. Therefore, the best way to keep evil spirits confused is to say what God said and do what the Word states.

1 Corinthians 14:2 For he that speaketh in an unknown tongue speaketh not unto men, but unto God: for no man understandeth him; howbeit in the spirit he speaketh mysteries.
(KJV)

My conversation with the Spirit of God started with Him answering some questions I had asked several days earlier. He was very specific, ensuring that each answer was clear. In His presence, you become very humble and aware of being saturated with love.

After answering my questions, He said, "I want you to buy Barbara an automobile." A few days before this conference, I had obtained a large sum of money which would have paid off our home. I had prayed for guidance in spending it wisely, and I still waited for an answer.

Now, I was hearing the Lord say to buy Barbara an automobile. I didn't want to, but I'd learned to be honest in God's presence. God knows our thoughts anyway. Besides, He is my Father and I can speak to Him as a son.

Why? I wondered. Since my wife did not help me establish Eagle Life Ministries, why should I buy her an automobile? Looking back over this event I believe this was the ultimate test of my love for God and my wife.

He repeated the request.

"Okay," I said. "I'll buy her a car if that's what you want."

For the next few minutes He gave me instructions about the purchase. No cheap vehicle, but one of equal value to

Introduction

I had been taught that these Scriptures gave me the right to order my wife around and that her job, as a godly woman, was to obey me. But what is the Holy Spirit saying to us? Let's find out first what the word "submit" means in this passage.

According to Thayer's Greek – English Lexicon of the New Testament, the word "submit" means to subject one's self, to obey; to submit to one's control; to yield to one's admonition or advice. The numerical code for the word "submit," according to Strong's Exhaustive Concordance, is "5293." In the case of the wife and the husband, the wife is to subject herself to her own husband. It is not something the husband forces her to do but a command she has been given by the Lord. The problem we have is defining words in a way that makes them conform to our requirements. What is the definition needed to suit my situation at the present time?

Ephesians 6:1-4 Children, obey your parents in the Lord: for this is right. Honour thy father and mother; (which is the first commandment with promise;) That it may be well with thee, and thou mayest live long on the earth. And, ye fathers, provoke not your children to wrath: but bring them up in the nurture and admonition of the Lord. (KJV)

There is another word used here for children which is "obey." Now, this is the word we want to use in Ephesians, Chapter 5, for the wife. But is this the same word? It isn't spelled or pronounced the same. What's the difference? The word "obey" means to hearken to a command, i.e., to obey, be obedient unto, submit to. This is a very strong word given to children in respect to their parents. The numerical code for the word "obey," in accordance the Strong's Exhaustive Concordance, is "5219."

The first thing we understand is that the words are different. They have two different numerical codes, according to Strong's Exhaustive Concordance, meaning they are not equivalent. This is a problem with the church as a whole. We have tried to put women in a box so we can dominate them. Man's nature is to rule. The problem is that God didn't give us ruler ship over one another.

Genesis 1:26-31 And God said, Let us make man in our image, after our likeness: and let them have dominion over the fish of the sea, and over the fowl of the air, and over the cattle, and over all the earth, and over every creeping thing that creepeth upon the earth. So God created man in his own image, in the image of God created he him; male and female created he them. And God blessed them, and God said unto them, Be fruitful, and multiply, and replenish the earth, and subdue it: and have dominion over the fish of the sea, and over the fowl of the air, and over every living thing that moveth upon the earth. And God said, Behold, I have given you every herb bearing seed, which is upon the face of all the earth, and every tree, in the which is the fruit of a tree yielding seed; to you it shall be for meat. And to every beast of the earth, and to every fowl of the air, and to every thing that creepeth upon the earth, wherein there is life, I have given every green herb for meat: and it was so. And God saw every thing that he had made, and, behold, it was very good. And the evening and the morning were the sixth day. (KJV)

You see the wife is not to be obedient to another man, and that is the problem with most marriages. God gave mankind dominion of mastery over the entire earth and all the animals upon it. But there wasn't any order given to man to rule over each other; man must submit to God. The Father God wants obedience from mankind. He and He alone.

There is a difference between the implication of the word 'submit" used for the wife and the word "obey" used for the children in Ephesians 6:1.

Introduction

A note of interest: the words "submitting" in Verse 21 and "subject" in Verse 24 have the same numerical code in accordance to Strong's Exhaustive Concordance. This sheds new light on what we have been taught in relation to the position of the wife. We are being told to submit to one another in Verse 21, in the fear of the Lord. And in Verse 24 we are told the wife is to "subject" to her husband as the church is subject to Christ in everything.

One of the greatest lessons we have to learn is the family should reflect the pattern of the Church of Christ. When most of us think about the church, we think about the structure of a local organization. When God speaks about the church, He is referring to you and me, the "called out ones," those who have accepted Jesus Christ as Lord and Savior. This is where I believe we have gone wrong.

Yes, the wife has a responsibility to submit to her husband. But how is she to submit? Is it like children are to obey their parents? Is it like a slave obeys his master? How do you want your wife to submit to you? Do you want her to be subject to you the way you submit to Christ?

The first local church we attended had a strong ministry in the area of submissiveness, not only between wife and husband but also between ministers and members. Men were taught to rule their home much like the military. As an ex – serviceman, I knew the drill. Now, I had a problem when the Holy Spirit began revealing the love of God to me.

We must understand the position of a wife and the position of a single woman. What we have done is placed all women in the same position. All Christians have the right to inform one another of the truth. Verse 21 said to submit yourselves one to another in the fear or reverence of God. It doesn't mean a woman cannot tell me the truth, even though we have used the Bible to make those claims. In Verse 22, Paul is trying to set some order to the family and keep other men from interfering. Therefore, he informs the wife she is to "submit herself" to the control of or counsel of her own husband.

The Lord began dealing with me about the word "love" used in these verses. You see, these verses were never taught to me the way I see them today. I believe one must understand the relationship between the Lord Jesus Christ and the Church before the true meaning of this scripture comes to light or, better still, the relationship between the Lord Jesus Christ and himself. It took me about ten years to understand truly God's method of love and how He deals with us. Why so long? Probably because I had been taught to dominate my wife and I liked it.

Ephesians 5:25-27 Husbands, love your wives, even as Christ also loved the church, and gave himself for it; That he might sanctify and cleanse it with the washing of water by the word, That he might present it to himself a glorious church, not having spot, or wrinkle, or any such thing; but that it should be holy and without blemish. (KJV)

I had been taught the word "love" in the above verse was the Greek word "agape." The numerical code for "love," according to Strong's Exhaustive Concordance, is "26." "Agape" is a noun defined as a spontaneous love, irrespective of rights. You see, the agape type of love is the highest form of love in the universe, obtainable only through the Holy Spirit.

I felt I had been operating in the agape mode. But to my surprise, mine was not the Greek meaning of the word "love" in that verse. The Greek verb "agapao" means "to regard with favor," "to make much of a thing or person", on principle, which is the numerical code 25.

I began to see that my responsibility was "to make much of my wife" and "to regard her with favor" at all times. It depended on me, the husband, to become like Christ is to the church, the called out ones. Thus began my walk toward forgiveness. Love has to be the basis for life. We cannot do things just because we hear someone teach it, or because we read it. It took me years to realize that I never really showed love correctly to my wife. I wonder how many of us suffer daily through relationships with our mates not mindful of this truth.

I continued to study and started practicing what the Spirit of God showed me. I made every effort to bring Barbara a gift when I traveled without her. Following God's commandment to me soon became a way of life. Love grows out of action. What you begin in faith becomes your desire. Faith without action is dead and you are dead without love.

Let me show you what really woke me up:

John 3:16 For God so loved the world, that he gave his only begotten Son, that whosoever believeth in him should not perish, but have everlasting life. (KJV)

Most people in the United States know or have heard this scripture and probably have become callous to it. As a Christian, I recite it automatically. But after my revelation about love, John 3:16 took on new light.

The word "love" in this verse is the same Greek word "agapao" meaning "to regard with favor," "to make much of a thing or person" is the same Greek word used in Ephesians which instructs the husband to love his wife. Therefore, God is saying He regards each of us with favor, and makes a lot over us by giving us His Son Jesus Christ. This is a special gift God gave to draw us to Himself. He doesn't try to make us accept Jesus; he freely offers this gift to us. The words are "whosoever believeth in him should not perish, but have everlasting life." He did not say we would be made to accept. In Verse 18, He states that those who believe not are condemned already. Therefore, we have a very good reason to accept Christ. But He does not force us to.

As a husband, I have been commanded by God to love my wife. That is my responsibility to Him. I learned this method works well with your enemies also. One pastor spoke against me to his congregation without cause, and the Spirit of God informed me to send him a financial gift. The accusations stopped and when I went to his church he introduced me to his congregation. God knows what will give your enemy peace with you and what will cause you to have peace.

Now someone will say, I did this same thing to my friend or mate and it didn't work. Well, you gave up too soon. How long are you to work the things of God? Until you change or the circumstance changes, and even then don't stop. You see, when it comes down to you and God, He is interested in everything about you. You are to do unto your neighbors as you do to yourself. Each of us must work on ourselves and then we will see the change.

The final Scripture that changed my life and caused me to forgive:

John 14:22-26 Judas saith unto him, not Iscariot, Lord, how is it that thou wilt manifest thyself unto us, and not unto the world? Jesus answered and said unto him, If a man love me, he will keep my words: and my Father will love him, and we will come unto him, and make our abode with him. He that loveth me not keepeth not my sayings: and the word which ye hear is not mine, but the Father's which sent me. These things have I spoken unto you, being yet present with you. But the Comforter, which is the Holy Ghost, whom the Father will send in my name, he shall teach you all things, and bring all things to your remembrance, whatsoever I have said unto you. (KJV)

My understanding of this Scripture is by disobeying the Word of God, we say, "Father God, we do not love you." But the attention getter for me states that He will not love us either. This means God is not going to make a lot to do over us if we do not make a lot to do over Him by obeying the Word.

Having nothing to do with His agape love for us, this particular set of verses puts you and me in a position to call the shots for our own lives. We can follow His Word and get Him on our side, or we can do what we want and be alone. When this revelation came to me, I set myself to walk in forgiveness and obedience.

CHAPTER I

CORRUPT COMMUNICATION DESTROYS THE DESIRE TO FORGIVE

Ephesians 4:29-32 Let no corrupt communication proceed out of your mouth, but that which is good to the use of edifying, that it may minister grace unto the hearers. And grieve not the holy Spirit of God, whereby ye are sealed unto the day of redemption. Let all bitterness, and wrath, and anger, and clamour, and evil speaking, be put away from you, with all malice: And be ye kind one to another, tenderhearted, forgiving one another, even as God for Christ's sake hath forgiven you. (KJV)

When considering corrupt communications, most of us think cursing and foul language. When I was growing up, none of the adults in our family used foul language. Mother wouldn't even let me say "dog –gone – it." We know that cursing and swearing is wrong, but there is another side of corrupt communication I want to address.

Webster's New World College Dictionary defines "corrupt" as changed from a sound condition to an unsound one;

spoiled; contaminated; rotten; morally unsound or debased; perverted; evil; depraved; errors.

Strong's Exhaustive Concordance indicates that word "corrupt" means rotten; worthless; bad. Therefore, slandering a person's name can be corrupt communication. Telling half – truths can destroy a person's future and career.

Think about the impact of words. When you hear "Russia, " what comes to mind? As a Christian, we should think about the field of souls ready for harvesting into the Kingdom of God. But anyone fifty years of age or older may have different views of the former Soviet Union, as some veterans view Vietnam. During the 1940s to the 1990s, the United States instilled in the minds of its citizenry, through the media, that the USSR was our enemy. Throughout this Cold War period, we poured trillions of dollars into military weaponry. The government indoctrinated us to hate peoples we didn't know and most of us had never seen.

It's scary to think how easily opinions can be swayed toward hatred and bitterness of strangers. The military taught me to fight and kill, while deep in my mind I was learning to kill Russians. Why? I didn't know any Russians until 1966.

While stationed in Germany from 1965 to 1968, a Russian worked for me. To tell you the truth, I didn't like the man and never knew why until I began writing this chapter. In retrospect I figured out the simple reason: because he was Russian. My thoughts were if Russia was so great, why didn't he go back there after the war. Why didn't the government teach me to hate the Germans? They killed millions of Jews and would have killed most Americans if they had succeeded in ruling the world.

The Cuban missile crisis probably triggered mass American prejudice against Russia. President John Kennedy halting Russian delivery of nuclear missiles and other weapons to Cuba nearly started a war between the U.S., Cuba and the USSR. We were told those ships carried missiles built to carry nuclear warheads. Forcing them to return to the Soviet Union without delivering the cargo was a great victory for us, America. At 18 years of age, I believed it was my responsibility to join the military to help keep America free. Most of the men on my father's side of the family were veterans: my grandfather, father, uncles. Now it was my turn.

I didn't understand at that time that bitterness and hatred were Satanic tools used to separate us. It doesn't matter who uses them, the results are the same. The media is one of the main tools used to indoctrinate one group of people against another. Governments use indoctrination very effectively to turn the public against the enemy they create. Professionally trained agents employ various means of communication to poison minds against individuals, products, political opponents, religious groups, races of people, etc.

The word "corrupt" means to degrade with unsound principles of moral values. The media has been used for years to corrupt the minds of U.S. citizens, creating racists and nationalists. Relentlessly, hammering us with lies leads to distrust and deceit.

Afro – Americans, Jews, Hispanics and many Asians have been targets of hatred for hundreds of years. What's the reason? Can anyone really come up with solid evidence to substantiate this action? Evil forces have existed among every race and nationality. But we must not forget that the media had never influenced or indoctrinated an entire population. Hitler with his SS troops and propaganda machine could not convince all Germans to kill Jews. God always has a remnant that will listen to the voice of the Holy Spirit.

This is true in the case of the United States. Many Caucasians lost their lives aiding slaves. Some were killed in the 1960s as they demonstrated with Black America for equality. Our forefathers who were enslaved, stripped of their identity, forced to provide free labor, sold as animals and misused at will wound up hated by descendants of their captors for hundreds of years.

America has a great price to pay for its cruelty and lack of compassion, not only to Black Americans but to Native Americans. Most of all, we must pay for the hatred instilled in the hearts and minds of our children. Consider this important point: when a person is taught to hate or think himself better than others for any reason, his mind is poisoned. It takes the Holy Spirit to set him free. As a product of the devil, hate causes us to turn on ourselves, eventually leading to our own destruction. Hate, a spiritual force, manifests itself as a sinful disease that eats up the carrier. It cannot be turned off and on at will. Once ignited, it spreads like wildfire, consuming everything in its path.

No one is beyond indoctrination, if there is a good motive. Throughout history nations have fought and killed because someone provided a reason. This is why the Bible tells us to guard our minds.

Esther 3:1-11 After these things did king Ahasuerus promote Haman the son of Hammedatha the Agagite, and advanced him, and set his seat above all the princes that were with him. And all the king's servants, that were in the king's gate, bowed, and reverenced Haman: for the king had so commanded concerning him. But Mordecai bowed not, nor did him reverence. Then the king's servants, which were in the king's gate, said unto Mordecai, Why transgressest thou the king's commandment? Now it came to pass, when they spake daily unto him, and he hearkened not unto them, that they told Haman, to see whether Mordecai's matters would stand: for he had told them that he was a Jew. And when Haman saw that Mordecai bowed not, nor did him reverence, then was Haman full of wrath. And he thought scorn to lay hands on Mordecai alone; for they had shewed him the people of Mordecai: wherefore Haman sought to destroy

Corrupt Communication Destroys The Desire To Forgive

all the Jews that were throughout the whole kingdom of Ahasuerus, even the people of Mordecai. In the first month, that is, the month Nisan, in the twelfth year of king Ahasuerus, they cast Pur, that is, the lot, before Haman from day to day, and from month to month, to the twelfth month, that is, the month Adar. And Haman said unto king Ahasuerus, There is a certain people scattered abroad and dispersed among the people in all the provinces of thy kingdom; and their laws are diverse from all people; neither keep they the king's laws: therefore it is not for the king's profit to suffer them. If it please the king, let it be written that they may be destroyed: and I will pay ten thousand talents of silver to the hands of those that have the charge of the business, to bring it into the king's treasuries. And the king took his ring from his hand, and gave it unto Haman the son of Hammedatha the Agagite, the Jews' enemy. And the king said unto Haman, The silver is given to thee, the people also, to do with them as it seemeth good to thee. (KJV)

    Haman created a reason to kill an entire race of people because he hated one man, Mordecia. He, like so many have done during our time, used his position to turn King Ahasuerus and his subjects against all Jewish people ... because he wanted to kill one man.

    Most of us have experienced or been the victim of corrupt communication used by someone to destroy our appreciation of another person. For example parents must be careful when advising their children not to associate with another child. Improper communication can cause a person to dislike another, when their real intent is just to warn against the person's bad character.

Esther 6:1 On that night could not the king sleep, and he commanded to bring the book of records of the chronicles; and they were read before the king. And it was found written, that Mordecai had told of Bigthana and Teresh, two of the king's chamberlains, the keepers of the door, who sought to lay hand on the king Ahasuerus. And the king said, What honour and dignity hath been done to Mordecai for this? Then said the king's servants that ministered unto him, There is nothing done for him. And the king said, Who is in the court? Now Haman was come into the outward court of the king's house, to speak unto the king to hang Mordecai on the gallows that he had prepared for him. And the king's servants said unto him, Behold, Haman standeth in the court. And the king said, Let him come in. So Haman came in. And the king said unto him, What shall be done unto the man whom the king delighteth to honour? Now Haman thought in his heart, To whom would the king delight to do honour more than to myself? And Haman answered the king, For the man whom the king delighteth to honour, Let the royal apparel be brought which the king useth to wear, and the horse that the king rideth upon, and the crown royal which is set upon his head: And let this apparel and horse be delivered to the hand of one of the king's most noble princes, that they may array the man withal whom the king delighteth to honour, and bring him on horseback through the street of the city, and proclaim before him, Thus shall it be done to the man whom the king delighteth to honour. Then the king said to Haman, Make haste, and take the apparel and the horse, as thou hast said, and do even so to Mordecai the Jew, that sitteth at the king's gate: let nothing fail of all that thou has spoken. Then took Haman the apparel and the horse, and arrayed Mordecai, and brought him on horseback through the street of the city, and proclaimed before him, Thus shall it be done unto the man whom the king delighteth to honour. And Mordecai came again to the king's gate. But Haman hasted to his house mourning, and having his head covered. And Haman told Zeresh his wife and all his friends every thing that had befallen him. Then said his wise men *and Zeresh his wife unto him, If Mordecai be of the seed of the Jews, before whom thou hast begun to fall, thou shalt not prevail against him, but shalt surely fall before him. And while they were yet talking with him, came the king's chamberlains, and hasted to bring Haman unto the banquet that Esther had prepared. (KJV)*

God normally steps forward to avenge those who honor Him. He will take the necessary measures to rectify a wrong done against a righteous person or people. In this case, God disturbed King Ahasuerus' sleep and moved him to read the book of records of the Chronicles. Mordecai was finally honored for saving the King's life.

Esther 7:2-10 And the king said again unto Esther on the second day at the banquet of wine, What is thy petition, queen Esther? and it shall be granted thee: and what is thy request? and it shall be performed, even to the half of the kingdom. Then Esther the queen answered and said, If I have found favour in thy sight, O king, and if it please the king, let my life be given me at my petition, and my people at my request: For we are sold, I and my people, to be destroyed, to be slain, and to perish. But if we had been sold for bondmen and bondwomen, I had held my tongue, although the enemy could not countervail the king's damage. Then the king Ahasuerus answered and said unto Esther the queen, Who is he, and where is he, that durst presume in his heart to do so? And Esther said, The adversary and enemy is this wicked Haman. Then Haman was afraid before the king and the queen. And the king arising from the banquet of wine in his wrath went into the palace garden: and Haman stood up to make request for his life to Esther the queen; for he saw that there was evil determined against him by the king. Then the king returned out of the palace garden into the place of the banquet of wine; and Haman was fallen upon the bed whereon Esther was. Then said the king, Will he force the queen also before me in the house? As the word went out of the king's mouth, they covered Haman's face. And Harbonah, one of the chamberlains, said before the king, Behold also, the gallows fifty cubits high, which Haman had made for Mordecai, who had spoken good for the king, standeth in the house of Haman. Then the king said, Hang him thereon. So they hanged Haman on the gallows that he had prepared for Mordecai. Then was the king's wrath pacified. (KJV)

It's amazing how a few leaders can incite a nation of people to kill their next door neighbors. These leaders used the principles of Mark 11:22 – 23 which are based on "saying" and "believing what is said," Verse 23 states, *"That whosoever shall say unto this mountain, Be thou removed, and be thou cast into the sea; and shall not doubt in his heart, but shall believe that those things which he saith shall come to pass; he shall have whatsoever he saith."*

These Scriptures are the foundation for the faith message. As in the above examples, we witness every day how nations continue to lead millions into hatred. They have taken the principles of God and are using them for Satanic means. This is happening all over the world.

The same principles apply when we deal with individuals. How many of us dislike a co – worker because of what others have said about that person? Some who have it in for someone corrupt the minds of others to follow suit because of envy and jealousy. If we say or hear something long enough, it becomes true to us. This is the reason God instructs us to study the Word of God day and night. He wants us to be indoctrinated with His Word, the absolute truth.

What is corrupt communication? The Amplified Bible gives us a good rendition of Ephesians 4:29, which answers this question: *"Let no corrupt communication proceed out of your mouth, but that which is good to the use of edifying,*

Corrupt Communication Destroys The Desire To Forgive

that it may minister grace unto the hearers." This indicates to me that negative worthless words said against others denote corrupt communication. Therefore, saying things about ourselves or others that are contrary to the Word of God is corrupt communication and, when heard often enough, becomes real to us.

Some years ago, I read that during World War II German missiles destroyed sections of England and terrorized the English people. But the English propaganda machine used the media to convince Germany that its missiles missed their targets. When this information reached the ears of Adolf Hitler, the leader of the Nazis and Chancellor of Germany pressured the scientists to make the necessary corrections. The type of communication transmitted and received can mean the difference between life and death.

A few years ago, we started receiving information revealing how the United States government used the Hollywood motion picture industry to pump the American people up for war. Today, we see international groups using the media to motivate our purchasing to further their financial means. The computer is another tool used to influence our thoughts. Unfortunately, there is little regulation or control over its use. These tools replace spiritual desires with carnal desires. People tend to believe what is communicated to them through the media, regardless of the credibility. A person of notable reputation informed me that the news is arranged to influence our way of thinking.

Unfortunately, it's difficult to convince people of the power of the spoken word. When I first heard the message of faith taught, and understood that I could really have what I said when I spoke in faith, I got excited. From that moment on, my goal was to line up my words with the Word of God and what I needed. My desires didn't come into the picture until years later, after I had met the many needs of my family.

Being armed with this new knowledge, I started using Biblical Scriptures that applied to my situation. I walked around the house saying, *"Philippians 4:19 But my God shall supply all your need according to his riches in glory by Christ Jesus."* At this time, I had difficulty tithing, giving offerings and paying my bills. Therefore, I felt like an idiot quoting Scriptures and seeing no results. Because we could not see into the Spiritual realm, I found myself operating in blind faith. But eventually, when words spoken in faith reached the Spiritual realm, the Kingdom of Heaven manifested the request into the physical realm.

I didn't know the process at the time, but now liken it to the growth of a seed. The seed is planted in the ground. During the day the sun gives heat and it cools off at night causing the seed to retract. All the time, it draws moisture from the ground, enabling it to develop into an embryo and burst through the seed's shell to germination. Within a few days, a blade emerges. Weeks later fruit is ready for harvest. This process works for all types of seeds, spiritual and physical. We must remember that every crop has to be nurtured for a season before reaping a harvest.

We should understand the principles of saying and believing. It takes work tending a crop. Nothing just happens by itself. Paul's statement in Philippians 4:19 was experimental. Action should accompany our faith, if we are to reach the same level of confidence in the Word of God he reached. Paul didn't allow the trials he endured to adversely affect his relationship with Jesus Christ or his belief in the Word of God. Remember, the level of confidence we have in Jesus and the Word of God will be produced by how we go through our trials.

In due season, God will show Himself to be faithful on your behalf, as He did in my life. When my season came, I was able to pay my tithes, offerings and bills with money left over for savings. I want to emphasize James 4:17 which tells us that faith, *"if it hath not works, it is dead, being alone."* Therefore, we must put our faith to work by doing whatever it takes to accomplish our God – given goals. As I continued this process, my words pulled me into their sphere of operation where I became their epistle. This is the reason God tells us to guard our mouths and not allow corrupt communication to proceed out of them.

In the early days of my spiritual life, I did not understand that things I experienced had a lot to do with what I said and heard. Regardless, if they were beneficial for me or not, they came into existence. This concept puzzles many because we are not accustomed to analyzing the Word of God with the laws of science of nature. You see, sown seeds will sprout in due time.

Storms and rain, or the lack thereof, doesn't just happen. We don't consider the jet stream, polluted air, reduction of trees, and other physical factors. But if we watch the weather or study meteorology and geography, we can see things affecting the weather and the earth.

The Father God showed us in the first Chapter of Genesis, the power of words as He spoke things into existence during the creation of the earth. When He said, *"Let there be light,"* it came into existence. He separated the waters into large and small bodies, seas and oceans by the spoken word. Most of us have no problem believing that God's Words would come to fruition, but we do not believe our own words carry similar power. As adopted children of God, we have the same type of power He has.

Romans 8:14-17 For as many as are led by the Spirit of God, they are the sons of God. For ye have not received the spirit of bondage again to fear; but ye have received the Spirit of adoption, whereby we cry, Abba, Father. The Spirit itself beareth witness with our spirit, that we are the children of God: And if children, then heirs; heirs of God, and joint-

heirs with Christ; if so be that we suffer with him, that we may be also glorified together. (KJV)

Our words are spiritual forces that govern and direct our lives. Spoken words determine what we are today and what we will become tomorrow. We have a choice as to what we accept as true. Be selective, filter out communications that will hinder you from reaching your maximum potential. Hearing is listening to and considering what is being said. Learn to hear effectively things that will build, not destroy, your relationship with the Lord Jesus Christ and others.

Some business people and pastors won't tolerate a negative speaking person on their staff. Someone bad – mouthing a person or a situation influences those around them to have doubt. Doubt carries power which can destroy plans of the pastor of a church or the president of a company. How correct the saying, "one bad apple can spoil the whole barrel." Most of us were taught by our parents to remove the spoiled ones to save the rest.

Speaking positively benefits the lives of those around us. Think about the difference between the spoken words "love" and "hate." A person saying "I love you" can change a bad mood to good. Those three words penetrate our entire being like warm sunshine on a cool autumn day. They comfort, give a feeling of acceptance, and make us feel good. "Love" softly spoken with a pleasant facial expression reveals affection.

On the other hand, the word "hate" registers a feeling of rejection. If we are the recipient of the phrase "I hate you", its force depresses our spirit. We want to know why the person hates us. These words cut like a knife. "Hate," a sharp and unkind word, implies we are not appreciated by a person whose eyes are cold and hard, forehead filled with wrinkles, face flushed and jaw tight.

Corrupt Communication Destroys The Desire To Forgive

Ephesians 4:29-32 Let no corrupt communication proceed out of your mouth, but that which is good to the use of edifying, that it may minister grace unto the hearers. And grieve not the holy Spirit of God, whereby ye are sealed unto the day of redemption. Let all bitterness, and wrath, and anger, and clamour, and evil speaking, be put away from you, with all malice: And be ye kind one to another, tenderhearted, forgiving one another, even as God for Christ's sake hath forgiven you. (KJV)

Corrupt communication destroys our desire to forgive because it continually presents the worst of a person or a situation. It was demonstrated above how governments and individuals used this method to develop ill will toward a people or another individual. We must reject negative comments that influence us to develop bitterness, wrath, anger, clamorous and evil speaking toward others. We must edify each other so that the Holy Spirit will not be grieved.

If we think and speak words that edify, we create the spirit of forgiveness. It's not normal for those of us who have accepted Jesus Christ as our Lord and Savior to hate. The foundation of the Spirit of God is love. God is love. Therefore, it is normal for us to operate in love because of the love of God in our hearts. It should be easier for a fish to live on dry land, than for a child of God to live in hate.

A woman I'll call Mrs. J was the most unpleasant person I had encountered during my 37 years in the workplace. She couldn't carry on a decent conversation without insulting you. Bitterness showed in her face and affected her personality. I believe the health problems she experienced came from that bitterness. Mrs. J's words worked against her every day. She sowed bitter seeds and reaped a bitter harvest. Everyone was glad when she retired. I tried to reach her, but couldn't get past her barrage of insults and complaints.

Thousands of bitter people have allowed evil spirits to take over their lives. These spirits are revealing themselves as they strive to destroy these people. Evil spirits possess and prevent you from functioning properly. When I was a child we knew this lady thought to be mentally ill. While talking to my mother and other ladies she'd suddenly attack them verbally and sometimes physically. I wondered why? Could corrupt communications have hardened her heart and mind?

As Christians, God gives us His requirements in His Word. Look at Ephesians 4:32: "*And be ye kind one to another, tenderhearted, forgiving one another, even as God for Christ's sake hath forgiven you.* " God set the example for us by forgiving us for Christ's sake. It appears that every person on earth can accept Christ, and God will forgive them of all their sins.

As Christians, we are required to forgive everyone's sins against us. What a job. Much more difficult to do than to write or preach. It takes effort to forgive. First of all, with the Holy Spirit as our helper, we must change our speech. No, everyone we forgive will not change, but we will. Keep in mind, after forgiving a person, you don't have to become best friends if there is no change in his life. The Bible tells us to stay away from those who don't walk godly before others.

The best way to defeat the devil: refuse him access to your mind. Don't let him know what you are thinking. Speak what the Bible says about your condition. Yes, this is hard at first because we feel like we're lying and our minds are not in line with the Word of God.

Let communications reveal your heart as standing on the Word of God in all situations. You are not alone. We all must live by the same rules.

CHAPTER II

FORGIVE AND FORGET

*I*n 1968 my wife and I became members of our first church as a family. It was a joy as the Word of God revealed to us our Lord and Savior Jesus Christ. Our pastor was a dynamic teacher who admonished us to dedicate at least an hour daily to studying the Word of God, and praying three times daily. The church also had a speech club which trained its men to properly present themselves before others. During our six years at that local church, I attended the speech club for five of those years. I graduated and started over again. I appreciated our pastor's ability to teach the Word of God with simplicity. Eventually, I was elected and trained for church leadership. We were taught how to study the Bible and how to deliver sermons. I believe God used those years to train me for what He has me doing today.

Over the years, the Holy Spirit led me into word studies, which shed new light on particular words in Scripture. As a teacher, it is my intent to present the Word of God as accurately as possible. Therefore, definitions from the Greek and Hebrew are important to me. To aid my studies, I invested thousands of dollars in Bible help books.

We need to understand what we teach. For instance, I know some people from England, and I spend much of our conversations trying to figure out what they're saying. The King James Version of the Bible, written in old English, is at times difficult to comprehend. This is the reason word study is important. King James must have known something about the Bible because he obeyed God's Old Testament commandment ordering each king to write the Bible for his nation in their own language.

I want to clarify some thoughts about two important words, "forget" and "forgive." First, Webster's New Collegiate Dictionary definitions:

Forget — to be unable to remember or call to mind: To treat with inattention; neglect; to fail or neglect to become aware of at the proper moment.

Forgive — to give up resentment against; to give up all claim to punish; to give up desire to punish; to cancel or remit a debt; stop being angry with.

Vine's Expository Dictionary of Old and New Testament Words defines the words as follows:

Forgive — to bestow a favor unconditionally; to let loose from; to release; to set a person free; denotes a dismissal.

Forget — to escape notice.

The definition of the word "forget" denotes something negative happening, loss of memory, being unable to remember or call to mind. Throughout the Scriptures, God reminds us not to forget His Word. He gave us methods to aid in remembering. It doesn't appear that forgetting is something we try to do but something happening because of

Forgive And Forget

neglect on our part. Of course, there are those who are mentally sick and have problems remembering.

Let's say, for example, that my wife calls me at the office and asks me to pick up a few items form the grocery on my way home from work. I arrived empty – handed. Why? Did I forget the information? Did what she asked me to do leave my mind? No, it simply wasn't thought of at the proper time. We remember events and information according to priority. What she requested was not at the top of my list then. Now, when she asks me to do something, I write it in my planner to make sure it's taken care of.

We have a saying in the work place, "a short pencil is better than a short memory." Some employees are notorious for entering their supervisor's office without pen or paper. This gives a bad impression of job performance. I learned in the military to write things down and carry them out to the letter.

A few weeks ago our department manager called me into his office to check the status of a particular project. I explained to him that none of his supervisors had taken action on the project. Immediately, he had his secretary summon them for a round of questioning. Not one remembered what they were supposed to have done. I noticed each one came into their manager's office without pen or paper. As a manager concluding they didn't consider what I said important, I would have adjusted their attitude.

Joshua 1:8 This book of the law shall not depart out of thy mouth; but thou shalt meditate therein day and night, that thou mayest observe to do according to all that is written therein: for then thou shalt make thy way prosperous, and then thou shalt have good success. (KJV)

Learn how your mind functions, so it will be of maximum benefit to you. The Word of God will help you prosper and give you the methods needed to obtain success.

We can say then that forgiveness is not forgetting. The one thing to remember is that man does not forget easily, but he should be quick to forgive. Forgiveness is essential for our health and sanity.

CHAPTER III

ONE OF THE DEVIL'S GREATEST LIES

The devil has many worldly leaders, Christian teachers and the church fathers believing this lie. *"If you have forgiven me, you would have forgotten it."* As you can see by the definitions of "forgive" and "forget" in the preceding chapter, there is a big difference between the two. Furthermore, people who forget everything are viewed as dumb or having mental problems. We don't expect anyone to remember everything, but if a person can't remember a particular event from the previous night, we would view that as a memory problem.

Another comment we hear a lot is, "I'll forgive but I'll never forget." There is truth in that statement. Forgetting is the process through which memorized information becomes inaccessible, either because it is no longer stored, or stored but not immediately retrievable. Forgetting may be increased by interference from other material, either learned beforehand or subsequently. In both cases, the amount of forgetting increases with the amount of interfering material, and with its similarity to what's being remembered. For example, if a cook tries to remember a soup recipe, recall will be worse if it is one of six soup recipes just read. On the other hand, reading a comparable amount of information about a different topic such as car maintenance might make it easier to recall the soup recipe.

Normally, persons who cannot remember a certain amount of information or experiences that occurred in his or her life are considered senile. God did not place a memory loss button in our minds to push anytime there's something we need to forget, although I have spoken with many young people who tell me they cannot remember their school work. My answer is always the same: do your school work after prayer and Bible study then the Holy Spirit will help you recall learned information. We must remember that these are the same young people who can recall every word of the latest rap songs. We notice sometimes memory is selective. People set priorities, and for some young people school work is not up there.

David B. Ellis in his book entitled *Becoming A Master Student* writes:

> Memory is the process of storing and retrieving information. Short term memory is the system used to remember information "in use," such as a telephone number while one is dialing it. Whether or not short term memory represents a separate system, it does have certain clearly defined characteristics. It is limited in storage capacity: most people can repeat a 7 or 8 digit telephone number, but not 10 or 11 digits. Short term memory appears to be related to speech. A string of similar sounding letters such as A U C I V T P is less likely to be remembered correctly than a string of dissimilar consonants such as K G R W F L. This phenomenon is not due to hearing incorrectly, because the effect also occurs when the letters are presented visually. It does, however, seem to depend on some form of inner speech, because congenitally deaf

children show the effect, provided they use speech reasonably well.

Memory is the power or process of reproducing or recalling what has been learned and retained especially through associative mechanisms. The memory part of the mind is very powerful, able to work better than any computer. It can receive and store information and experiences, and then compare the information and experiences collected, allowing us to make proper decisions. The mind has long term and short term memory. The things that we learn over a period of continual use will stay with us, stored in our long term memory.

For example: I remember the service number given to me when I entered the military in 1962. The main reason is because of continual use. Another example is our Social Security number, which most people know.

David B. Ellis further states:

> Sensory memory is the process of perceiving, and often involves accumulating information during a period of time. Hearing a sentence, a word, or even a syllable requires the listener to integrate a changing pattern of auditory stimulation. This integration demands some form of temporary buffer storage, and it is fairly certain that perception relies heavily on such temporary memory stores. It is also clear that humans have long term memory, for sensory information, for the sound of a violin, the taste of an apple, or the color of a sunset. Such information is stored in some relatively permanent form; whether different sensory modalities are stored separately, or whether they form part of a more general memory store, is unclear.

The Healing and Peace of Forgiveness

There are also events that are stamped in our memory which we will never forget. Hurt, pain, death, fear, etc., are active events that will stay with us. God began giving me revelation which dispels the theory, if you have forgiven me you would have forgotten, after my brother passed some years ago. I would be driving along and start crying uncontrollably. This went on for at least a week before the pain of his death subsided. I place this in the category of sensory memory.

You see, the death of my brothers and my father and the events surrounding their death will never be forgotten. The pain from those events is no longer present, but this information is stored permanently in my mind. The reason so many people go to the altar for prayer when a minister teaches forgiveness is because their rationale is "I remember the incident so I haven't forgiven the person yet." The event is not forgotten, and they associate remembering with unforgiveness. They feel if the event is remembered, they have not forgiven. This is not necessarily true.

I don't want you to think I look over the fact that some people live with hatred and have not forgiven. There are some incidents we will never forget. But we must forgive those who have done us wrong. We don't have to trust them until they've proven themselves trustworthy. Because a person is not trustworthy and you don't trust him, does not mean you have not forgiven the person.

Remember, God created us to remember. The word "remember" is used by God hundreds of times throughout the Bible, instructing us to remember His Word. God has given us the Holy Spirit to help us through difficult times. God created in us a natural process that removes the pain of hurt and allows healing to take place. We are then able to minister to others with similar problems. Experiences help develop our abilities to minister.

We must remember that every hurt takes time to heal. There is a physical, mental and spiritual process to healing. We may have forgiven and still feel the pain. Do not be moved by those feelings, but continue to walk in the spirit of forgiveness. Do not hold resentment or a desire to see the person get paid back.

Some things you see go into your short term memory, and then they are gone. We see a house; the yard is beautiful but we cannot describe it later. Another good example: I told my wife about having met a person at the store. She asked what he wore. I couldn't say because it was not of interest to me. I did know the person was dressed, and by concentrating I may have recalled more.

What most people do not understand is that once information is stored into the memory, it is never lost. Sometimes, however, we may have difficulty recalling that information. I heard one person describe the memory as a maze with a lot of places to hide information. There are people who have had traumatic experiences, who hide not only their experiences but themselves in sections of those mazes. They are considered mentally unstable.

Philippians 3:13-14 Brethren, I count not myself to have apprehended: but this one thing I do, forgetting those things which are behind, and reaching forth unto those things which are before, I press toward the mark for the prize of the high calling of God in Christ Jesus. (KJV)

Here God tells us, through the Apostle Paul, to forget the things behind us and reach for the things before us. We will never reach the goal or purpose of our ministry or lives looking behind at our negative experiences. The word "forgetting" in this verse means "to neglect" or "to no longer care for." When we move toward the light of God's Word, those negative experiences behind us will not matter. This

The Healing and Peace of Forgiveness

verse is not saying to lose the memory of our experiences. The Apostle Paul used his experiences all the time to minister to people.

Acts 9:1-9 And Saul, yet breathing out threatenings and slaughter against the disciples of the Lord, went unto the high priest, And desired of him letters to Damascus to the synagogues, that if he found any of this way, whether they were men or women, he might bring them bound unto Jerusalem. And as he journeyed, he came near Damascus: and suddenly there shined round about him a light from heaven: And he fell to the earth, and heard a voice saying unto him, Saul, Saul, why persecutest thou me? And he said, Who art thou, Lord? And the Lord said, I am Jesus whom thou persecutest: it is hard for thee to kick against the pricks. And he trembling and astonished said, Lord, what wilt thou have me to do? And the Lord said unto him, Arise, and go into the city, and it shall be told thee what thou must do. And the men which journeyed with him stood speechless, hearing a voice, but seeing no man. And Saul arose from the earth; and when his eyes were opened, he saw no man: but they led him by the hand, and brought him into Damascus. And he was three days without sight, and neither did eat nor drink. (KJV)

I believe all of our experiences can be used to bring healing to those crossing our path.

CHAPTER IV

THE SORE THAT MUST BE HEALED

2 Corinthians 12:9-10 And he said unto me, My grace is sufficient for thee: for my strength is made perfect in weakness. Most gladly therefore will I rather glory in my infirmities, that the power of Christ may rest upon me. Therefore I take pleasure in infirmities, in reproaches, in necessities, in persecutions, in distresses for Christ's sake: for when I am weak, then am I strong. (KJV)

*I*f you cut a plug out of your finger, a few days later you'll see signs of healing. Then formation of a scab, the true indication the body's healing process is working. If properly protected, the injury heals within a few weeks. The scab falls off and new skin covers the area.

However, if the same area of that finger is damaged again within a few days and the scab is broken or lacerated, the healing process must start anew. As long as the person works with the finger unprotected and in the same situation which led to the initial damage, it will not heal. Such neglect could cause serious problems.

The same principle applies to the spiritual or mental healing process. When we forgive someone who hurts us, the ill feeling about the incident may not leave for some months. However, if we allow the healing process time to work, the hurt leaves and we grow well again. God created us to experience pain and hurt, but just for a short time. Once the pain leaves, the person uses the finger as if nothing happened. After a period of time, the pain is only a memory with no adverse side affects such as bitterness and hatred.

You must understand that we do have the Holy Spirit to protect us here on earth. He will give us knowledge for handling situations, but will never force us to follow that knowledge. Most Christians think they have faith to stand in situations — as the following example — but most don't. We don't walk in faith long enough during a normal day to always be protected by the Spirit. In other words, we get over our heads and refuse wise counseling. Similar circumstances happening to so many spouses make this case common in today's society.

"Annie" was living, by choice, in an unprotected situation. Hearing her husband's lies, she knew he often left the house to visit one of his lady friends. It got to the point she didn't know when he was lying or telling the truth. She indicated to me she was going through the same thing as Paul and felt she was standing like him. She also thought it her responsibility to stay in this situation to show her self as a strong Christian.

But the hurt became too much and soon turned into bitterness. Over the years the bitterness turned into hate. It was like the unprotected finger being continually re-injured, an open sore without a scab. There wasn't enough time between incidents for Annie to heal before the sore got opened again. This is a trying situation to live in daily.

One thing I want to point out here: Annie's husband was a good provider and did not physically abuse her. It appeared he actually loved her but found himself caught up with the spirit of lust. Believe me, there are many of you reading this book that are fighting that same spirit of lust.

My advice to Annie: get out of those conditions and pray for God to change your husband. You see, it's easier to pray for a person who isn't adversely affecting you. Annie decided to stay. I'm sure the security and comfort he provided influenced her decision. This is not an isolated case; thousands of women live in much worse conditions. I know this as the work of Satan; when some men achieve wealth, they turn to adultery. Maybe that's why James was so hard on the rich of his day. Many of them were evil men.

James 5:1-6 Go to now, ye rich men, weep and howl for your miseries that shall come upon you. Your riches are corrupted, and your garments are motheaten. Your gold and silver is cankered; and the rust of them shall be a witness against you, and shall eat your flesh as it were fire. Ye have heaped treasure together for the last days. Behold, the hire of the labourers who have reaped down your fields, which is of you kept back by fraud, crieth: and the cries of them which have reaped are entered into the ears of the Lord of sabaoth. Ye have lived in pleasure on the earth, and been wanton; ye have nourished your hearts, as in a day of slaughter. Ye have condemned and killed the just; and he doth not resist you. (KJV)

This is not only for Christians but also for the rich who act in this manner. Some ministers have obtained riches and love their riches — working for the money, not to minister to God's people. If this applies to you, repent and God will forgive.

Annie's case did not end here. She began hating her husband. As we know, Satan will not stop with just victory over a situation; he wants to destroy the entire person. Annie developed a hatred for men in general until she could not accept their wisdom or help. Her hatred would destroy even her grandchildren and their relationship with their parents. Hatred is one of the most destructive, divisive forces of the devil.

Please believe me when I say this is very common today. A minister and his wife did the same thing to their daughter and son-in-law. They agreed with the sinful acts of their granddaughter to win her over from her parents. The mother when confronted stated to her daughter; you ran away from home when you were a teenager. She had never forgiven her for leaving. A guest speaker in one of our local churches stated that her mother did the same thing to win her granddaughter. Remember the devil has no new tricks. He plays the same ones over and over again. The sad part is that most Christians don't know enough of the Word of God to see it coming and defeat him.

It happened I was with Annie's husband the day before he died of cancer. I asked him if he had accepted Jesus Christ as his Savior. He became very upset and said I hurt his feelings. I responded that I wanted to make sure he was right with God. I hate to say it, but in my opinion this man was not saved. That same day his girlfriend's brother came to the room and got some money for his sister. It's hard for me to understand what goes through the mind of a person who knows he is dying and still won't accept Christ.

One thing that may put some light on this case is this man's pastor told him everything would be all right. He even gave him communion. Ministers, we must understand that being a member of a church, and paying our dues, and being water baptized, does not save us. This type of teaching will send people to hell, even you.

Annie is living today with this same hatred. Her husband died, and if she doesn't get rid of the hate, she will follow him. We cannot live with hatred for any reason. Open sores will kill. If you have an open sore, continue to read this book and let God minister to your needs. If you're serious, pray the following, God will hear and heal you.

> God, I am a sinner. Please forgive me of my sins against you. I ask Jesus Christ to come into my life and be my Lord and Savior. Thank you, Father God. Now, Father, from this day on I will serve you and Jesus Christ, I will be quick to forgive others and pray that you will help me to be merciful to those I come into contact with daily. Thank you, Father God in Jesus name. Amen

Once you have accepted Christ as your Lord and Savior, these verses are for you.

1 John 1:8-9 If we say that we have no sin, we deceive ourselves, and the truth is not in us. If we confess our sins, he is faithful and just to forgive us our sins, and to cleanse us from all unrighteousness. If we say that we have not sinned, we make him a liar, and his word is not in us.
1 John 2:1 My little children, these things write I unto you, that ye sin not. And if any man sin, we have an advocate with the Father, Jesus Christ the righteous: 2 And he is the propitiation for our sins: and not for ours only, but also for the sins of the whole world. (KJV)

As the Scriptures show, none of us is without sin. Sin means to miss the mark. Jesus has paid the price and given His blood so that we can repent of the sins we have committed. Through God's faithfulness we will be forgiven. The blood of Jesus will wash away all of our sins. Annie has heard this many times, but I wonder if she really understands the true meaning of the blood of Jesus.

You may be in the same position as Annie and feel God cannot or will not forgive you. Well, I am here to tell you that

The Healing and Peace of Forgiveness

God will forgive you. He is waiting for you to say, "Father God, please forgive me for my sins and clean me." Then, ask Jesus Christ to come into your life and be your Lord and Savior. Ask the Father God to allow the Holy Spirit to live in you and direct you. Pray the above prayer earnestly, from your heart, and God the Father will hear.

You must understand the provision for salvation has been made available to us for over two thousand years. Jesus is our advocate with the Father. We are not able to be our own advocate because of the sin nature we received from Adam. Forgiveness is the nature of God, one of His powerful spiritual forces, just as un-forgiveness is a spiritual force of Satan. God is love, and peace comes with the spiritual force of forgiveness. We must allow that force to act within us.

Psalms 32:1-2 Blessed is he whose transgression is forgiven, whose sin is covered. Blessed is the man unto whom the LORD imputeth not iniquity, and in whose spirit there is no guile. (KJV)

Many Bible Scriptures show God the Father wants to and will forgive us. Remember, if you think you are not forgiven, your prayers will be hindered. You must accept the provisions that God has supplied through Jesus Christ's blood.

Philippians 3:13-16 Brethren, I count not myself to have apprehended: but this one thing I do, forgetting those things which are behind, and reaching forth unto those things which are before, I press toward the mark for the prize of the high calling of God in Christ Jesus. Let us therefore, as many as be perfect, be thus minded: and if in any thing ye be otherwise minded, God shall reveal even this unto you. Nevertheless, whereto we have already attained, let us walk by the same rule, let us mind the same thing. (KJV)

The Sore That Must Be Healed

Some things we must let go of and move on. Paul said to forget those things which are behind, and reach forth unto those things which are ahead of us. Even Annie's children still love her and pray for her; they are Christians and don't hold anything against her. They understand the power of the enemy. They also know the power of forgiveness and the destructive force behind un-forgiveness.

All Christians have a great goal to press toward the prize of the high calling of God which is in Christ Jesus. I say to all the Annie's reading this book: "Let us therefore, as many as be perfect, be thus minded: and if in any thing ye be otherwise minded, God shall reveal even this unto you. Nevertheless, whereto we have already attained, let us walk by the same rule, let us mind the same thing."

God is the healer.

CHAPTER V

EFFECT AND HEALING OF BROKEN RELATIONSHIPS

Eph 4:26-27 Be ye angry, and sin not: let not the sun go down upon your wrath: Neither give place to the devil. (KJV)

From childhood we are taught to strike back at anyone who hurts or offends us. In most cases, it doesn't matter if the statement considered offensive is right or wrong; it's what we believe that counts. People are so angry these days. Nothing satisfies them, and everything infuriates them, and any little incident pushes them over the edge.

But to be honest with you, they will never be happy without accepting Jesus Christ as Lord and Savior.

I love to walk and pray; that is the time the Father God can reach me. My mind is open to receive from the Spirit and listen. I had tried to figure out a way to improve my relationship with the Father God, and to see the progress.

He reminded me of my military buddies. We would do nearly anything for one another. One weekend I went to see if a friend wanted to go to the NCO club with me. His wife invited me in and informed me he wasn't home. Then she tried to seduce me. I would not submit to her desires and left.

Why? For starters, I had a wife, and her husband as a best friend. Now you must remember, I was not a Christian at that stage in my life. Therefore, I believe the Father God said to me, my relationship with Him should be greater than the one with my buddies. Developing a deep relationship with the Father God causes us to think before operating in lust. It gives us a reason to obey.

Sure, we'll get angry, but we mustn't allow that anger to turn into hatred or animosity. Hatred actually means "to have an emotion or extreme dislike or malice" or "animosity towards another person." Never let hatred become a part of you because it will open you up for evil forces causing spiritual, mental and physical problems. Those traits of Satan are designed to develop in you a seed of un-forgiveness.

Let's look at the word "anger" in Ephesians 4:26. It means "to provoke, arouse to anger, to be provoked to anger." Vine's Expository Dictionary tells us "anger" implies "the first keenness of the sense of provocation must not be cherished, though righteous resentment may remain." The Companion Bible says "anger" implies "righteous indignation." God is saying that anger is not a sin, unless held in the mind long enough to develop into wrath.

Wrath is the key word we need to focus on in this verse. Webster's New World College Dictionary defines "wrath" as intense anger, rage, and fury, any action carried out in great anger, especially for punishment or vengeance. Vine's Expository Dictionary: the Greek word "thumos," wrath, indicates a more agitated condition of the feelings, as outbursts of wrath from inward indignation, while anger suggests a more settled or abiding condition of mind, frequently with a view to taking revenge, although it does not necessarily include it.

Our thoughts are like seeds; the more we meditate and think about a thing, the more it develops. The more you think about a wrong done to you, the more energy it takes from you to feed it. After a while, it consumes your life. The anger has all the energy needed to turn into wrath, which will develop into hatred. The mind becomes clouded with hate, and a small offense done against you turns into a major event. Now you are ready to fight, kill, or separate from the person who offended you. This type of behavior could lead to demonic possession.

Prolonged meditation causes what you're meditating on to become a part of you and you to become a part of it. It takes over your life. This is the reason God tells us to meditate on His Word day and night. He wants us to become part of the Word and His Word to become part of us.

Remember, the devil is not a respecter of persons. He will use us in any way he can, if we allow him to influence our minds. When you are in a relationship with a person or a group of people, you can accomplish nearly anything. Whether in the ministry or in a business, the results will be the same: successful. This is one reason Satan strives to destroy our relationships with those we love.

There are broken relationships that occur between pastors and their congregations, parents and children, employers and employees, and friends. I'd venture to say, everyone has experienced at least one broken relationship.

Some have more than one a day. What happens if that person is in a position of authority such as a world leader, a pastor, a member of your congregation, a staff worker, an employer, an employee, your mate, a child, or your parent? We must become aware of these occurrences happening to us and those around us. With this knowledge, we can release anger and mend relationships instead of destroying them.

I believe every incident leading to a broken relationship adversely affects a person's attitude. Let's look at the definitions of "relationship:"

Effect And Healing Of Broken Relationships

- ❖ The state of being related or interrelated.
- ❖ The relation connecting or binding participants in a relationship: kinship; a specific instance or type of kinship.
- ❖ A state of affairs existing between those having relations or dealings: a romantic or passionate attachment; having a good relationship with a friend or family.

Disturbance or disruption of a relationship with any of these groups causes mental stress. If it is disrupted by death or violence, the stress level will be higher. Many things we have no control over, but when a broken relationship occurs with some group in which we are involved or our family, the picture is different. Often someone gets hurt or angry. In these cases someone needs to reconcile the difference; otherwise, un-forgiveness will govern the situation.

In general, most un-forgiveness stems from some form of broken relationship. It started with Adam and Eve in the garden God planted eastward in Eden. God warned Adam that eating from the Tree of Knowledge of Good and Evil would surely result in death. The very day Adam ate the forbidden fruit, he died spiritually, destroying his direct contact with God. God said a day was as a thousand years and a thousand years was as a day. Though God created man to live forever, Adam didn't even live a thousand years.

Adam and Eve rebelled against God and ate the fruit from the Tree of Knowledge. This first recorded sin of man broke his relationship with the Father. Afterwards, God removed from man the awareness of His presence. Adam and Eve's act not only separated them from God, but it separated the entire human race from having an intimate relationship with God the Father, until after Jesus. Now we have the right to develop a relationship with the Father God, through Jesus Christ.

The Healing and Peace of Forgiveness

Romans 5:14-15 Nevertheless death reigned from Adam to Moses, even over them that had not sinned after the similitude of Adam's transgression, who is the figure of him that was to come. But not as the offence, so also is the free gift. For if through the offence of one many be dead, much more the grace of God, and the gift by grace, which is by one man, Jesus Christ, hath abounded unto many. KJV

We have been delivered from the curse of the law, but we have not been removed from the influence of the world. Therefore, we have to be aware of our actions when people do contrary things to us. One shining example of this principle is the life of Joseph, the son of Jacob.

Genesis 37:3-18 Now Israel loved Joseph more than all his children, because he was the son of his old age: and he made him a coat of many colours. And when his brethren saw that their father loved him more than all his brethren, they hated him, and could not speak peaceably unto him. And Joseph dreamed a dream, and he told it his brethren: and they hated him yet the more. And he said unto them, Hear, I pray you, this dream which I have dreamed: For, behold, we were binding sheaves in the field, and, lo, my sheaf arose, and also stood upright; and, behold, your sheaves stood round about, and made obeisance to my sheaf. And his brethren said to him, Shalt thou indeed reign over us? or shalt thou indeed have dominion over us? And they hated him yet the more for his dreams, and for his words. And he dreamed yet another dream, and told it his brethren, and said, Behold, I have dreamed a dream more; and, behold, the sun and the moon and the eleven stars made obeisance to me. And he told it to his father, and to his brethren: and his father rebuked him, and said unto him, What is this dream that thou hast dreamed? Shall I and thy mother and thy brethren indeed come to bow down ourselves to thee to the earth? And his brethren envied him; but his father observed the saying. And his brethren went to feed their father's flock in Shechem. And Israel said unto Joseph, Do not thy brethren feed the flock in Shechem? come, and I will send thee unto them. And he said to him, Here am I. And he said to him, Go, I pray thee, see whether it be well with thy brethren, and well with the flocks; and bring me word again. So he sent him out of the vale of Hebron, and he came to Shechem. And a certain man found him, and, behold, he was wandering in the field: and the man asked him, saying, What seekest thou? And he said, I seek my brethren: tell me, I pray thee, where they feed their flocks. And the man said, They are departed hence; for I heard them say, Let us go to Dothan. And Joseph went after his brethren, and found them in Dothan. And when they saw him afar off, even before he came near unto them, they conspired against him to slay him. KJV

    Joseph's father loved him more than his other children, because he was the son of his old age. That was a mistake. Jacob, the father of Joseph, allowed his other children to know that his heart was toward his younger son. This caused his other sons to develop such resentment that they wanted to kill Joseph and made plans to do so.

    Their relationship was destroyed the day their father gave Joseph the coat of many colors. I Corinthians 3:3 tell us the traits of a carnal person: full of envy, strife, and one who walks in division. In other words, envy is the same as jealousy or resentment. A spirit of fear comes over a person who feels he is going to be replaced. I believe many children have that feeling when a brother or sister is born. It is the responsibility of the parents to ensure the older child they are as loved as their younger brother or sister. Jacob did not understand this principle. As a result, he endured pain and heartache for years. This incident stayed with him until the day he died. We can tell this by his deathbed blessing of his son Joseph.

Genesis 49:1-33 And Jacob called unto his sons, and said, Gather yourselves together, that I may tell you that which shall befall you in the last days.
2 Gather yourselves together, and hear, ye sons of Jacob; and hearken unto Israel your father. Reuben, thou art my firstborn, my might, and the beginning of my strength, the excellency of dignity, and the excellency of power: Unstable as water, thou shalt not excel; because thou wentest up to thy father's bed; then defiledst thou it: he went up to my couch. Simeon and Levi are brethren; instruments of cruelty are in their habitations. O my soul, come not thou into their secret; unto their assembly, mine honour, be not thou united: for in their anger they slew a man, and in their selfwill they digged down a wall. Cursed be their anger, for it was fierce; and their wrath, for it was cruel: I will divide them in Jacob, and scatter them in Israel. Judah, thou art he whom thy brethren shall praise: thy hand shall be in the neck of thine enemies; thy father's children shall bow down before thee. Judah is a lion's whelp: from the prey, my son, thou art gone up: he stooped down, he couched as a lion, and as an old lion; who shall rouse him up? The sceptre shall not depart from Judah, nor a lawgiver from between his feet, until Shiloh come; and unto him shall the gathering of the people be. Binding his foal unto the vine, and his ass's colt unto the choice vine; he washed his garments in wine, and his clothes in the blood of grapes: His eyes shall be red with wine, and his teeth white with milk. Zebulun shall dwell at the haven of the sea; and he shall be for an haven of ships; and his border shall be unto Zidon. Issachar is a strong ass couching down between two burdens: And he saw that rest was good, and the land that it was pleasant; and bowed his shoulder to bear, and became a servant unto tribute. Dan shall judge his people,

as one of the tribes of Israel. Dan shall be a serpent by the way, an adder in the path, that biteth the horse heels, so that his rider shall fall backward. I have waited for thy salvation, O LORD. Gad, a troop shall overcome him: but he shall overcome at the last. Out of Asher his bread shall be fat, and he shall yield royal dainties. Naphtali is a hind let loose: he giveth goodly words. Joseph is a fruitful bough, even a fruitful bough by a well; whose branches run over the wall: The archers have sorely grieved him, and shot at him, and hated him: But his bow abode in strength, and the arms of his hands were made strong by the hands of the mighty God of Jacob; (from thence is the shepherd, the stone of Israel:) Even by the God of thy father, who shall help thee; and by the Almighty, who shall bless thee with blessings of heaven above, blessings of the deep that lieth under, blessings of the breasts, and of the womb: The blessings of thy father have prevailed above the blessings of my progenitors unto the utmost bound of the everlasting hills: they shall be on the head of Joseph, and on the crown of the head of him that was separate from his brethren. Benjamin shall ravin as a wolf: in the morning he shall devour the prey, and at night he shall divide the spoil. All these are the twelve tribes of Israel: and this is it that their father spake unto them, and blessed them; every one according to his blessing he blessed them. And he charged them, and said unto them, I am to be gathered unto my people: bury me with my fathers in the cave that is in the field of Ephron the Hittite, In the cave that is in the field of Machpelah, which is before Mamre, in the land of Canaan, which Abraham bought with the field of Ephron the Hittite for a possession of a buryingplace. There they buried Abraham and Sarah his wife; there they buried Isaac and Rebekah his wife; and there I buried Leah. The purchase of the field and of the cave that is therein was from the children of Heth. And when Jacob had made an end of commanding his sons, he gathered up his feet into the bed, and yielded up the ghost, and was gathered unto his people. KJV

When envy or jealousy takes hold of a person, strife will soon follow. Strife means contention, competition, quarrel, conflict and struggle. You can believe Jacob's sons quarreled to gain his favor. If your children always quarrel with each other, let them know you love each of them equally. Unfortunately, today many children turn to gangs for comfort, attention, and security.

Most people who feel isolated share a tendency to come together. The sons of Jacob came together against Joseph and their father Jacob. Their attitude toward Joseph broke their relationship with the entire family. You cannot hurt one without hurting all in a family.

When envy and strife begin working in our lives, division is always the next problem. Division is the act of disagreeing, having a difference of opinion, or separating into groups. This is what the sons of Jacob did. Remember, only two of these sons had the same mother. Joseph's mother was named Rachel and his brother was Benjamin.

Another point I want to bring out here is that Jacob had two wives and a few handmaidens by whom he had children. Some of the sons of handmaidens probably felt a little inferior to their brothers. When a person suffers from inferiority, they sometimes become critical of others. This created the ideal climate for the devil to become involved and to assist them in forming a hate group. The foundation had been laid to escalate the plan for Joseph's murder.

Satan had not forgotten the command God had spoken in the garden of Eden. The Lord God informed Satan that the seed of the woman would bruise his head. Satan did not know who the man would be, so he tried to eliminate every man that appeared as though he could be the Savior. The condition was now right for the brothers of Joseph to put their plan into action.

Genesis 37:20-36 Come now therefore, and let us slay him, and cast him into some pit, and we will say, Some evil beast hath devoured him: and we shall see what will become of his dreams. And Reuben heard it, and he delivered him out of their hands; and said, Let us not kill him. And Reuben said unto them, Shed no blood, but cast him into this pit that is in the wilderness, and lay no hand upon him; that he might rid him out of their hands, to deliver him to his father again. And it came to pass, when Joseph was come unto his brethren, that they stript Joseph out of his coat, his coat of many colours that was on him; And they took him, and cast him into a pit: and the pit was empty, there was no water in it. And they sat down to eat bread: and they lifted up their eyes and looked, and, behold, a company of Ishmeelites came from Gilead with their camels bearing spicery and balm and myrrh, going to carry it down to Egypt. And Judah said unto his brethren, What profit is it if we slay our brother, and conceal his blood? Come, and let us sell him to the Ishmeelites, and let not our hand be upon him; for he is our brother and our flesh. And his brethren were content. Then there passed by Midianites merchantmen; and they drew and lifted up Joseph out of the pit, and sold Joseph to the Ishmeelites for twenty pieces of silver: and they brought Joseph into Egypt. And Reuben returned unto the pit; and, behold, Joseph was not in the pit; and he rent his clothes. And he returned unto his brethren, and said, The child is not; and I, whither shall I go? And they took Joseph's coat, and killed a kid of the goats, and dipped the coat in the blood; And they sent the coat of many colours, and they brought it to their father; and said, This have we found: know now whether it be thy son's coat or no. And he knew it, and said, It is my son's coat; an evil beast hath devoured him; Joseph is without doubt rent in pieces. And Jacob rent his clothes, and put sackcloth upon his loins, and mourned for his son many days. And all his sons and all his daughters rose up to comfort him; but he refused to be comforted; and he said, For I will go down into the grave unto my son mourning. Thus his father wept for him. And the Midianites sold him into Egypt unto Potiphar, an officer of Pharaoh's, and captain of the guard. KJV

Reuben, who didn't go along with the plot to kill Joseph, convinced his brothers to put him into a pit, hoping to come back later and return him to his father. When Judah saw the Ishmeelites, he got an idea to sell Joseph and make some money.

Verse 29 says Reuben returned to get Joseph out of the pit, but he wasn't there and he tore his clothes in anguish. This showed the pain of Reuben who, as the oldest brother, carried the responsibility for the safety of all his brothers. This broken relationship caused a father to mourn for his son until they reunited many years later.

We must not allow the feelings of others to influence us or lure us into their evil actions. Reuben was like many today who go along with the program while planning to pull out at the last minute.

2 Corinthians 10:2-6 For though we live in the world, we do not wage war as the world does. The weapons we fight with are not the weapons of the world. On the contrary, they have divine power to demolish strongholds. We demolish arguments and every pretension that sets itself up against the knowledge of God, and we take captive every thought to make it obedient to Christ. And we will be ready to punish every act of disobedience, once your obedience is complete. NIV

The Holy Spirit gave us another example through the Apostle Paul of how to handle ungodly situations. Thoughts and pain can develop into strongholds in our lives. Strongholds are like ancient walled cities in Europe or an outlaw's hideout in the old western movies –places hard to get into without permission.

In our minds strongholds have been developing over the years. They may be anything from the way we think, to how we respond to people of different races. God says we must not war against these things with the flesh, but with weapons that are mighty through God to the pulling down of these strongholds. Our most powerful weapons are the Word of God and prayer.

Learning and obeying the Word of God gives us the power and ability to cast down imaginations. When we cast down something, we throw it down, pull it down or demolish it completely. When I was a child in North Carolina, I worked in the peanut fields. During harvest we had to place the peanut vines on poles so they could dry out. We put a pole into the ground and nailed two four feet long strips of wood, approximately two inches in diameter, in a cross at the bottom, forming a crude platform where we stacked the vines.

Workers plowed up the plants a day or two before stacking them. This allowed the serpents and other small animals in to hunt rats that fed on the peanuts. Many times when picking up a handful of vines, a serpent fell out. Each time, I cast those vines down. It got so bad in one field, I couldn't work for fear of the serpents. This experience gave me a good understanding of the phrase "casting down."

This is what God wants us to do to imaginations. Imaginations are reasoning, judgement, decisions, or thoughts that exalt or elevate themselves above the knowledge of God. I attended a meeting with some people one day and saw this principle operating. The manager began discussing something negative as though it would happen. I didn't see how it could, but in his mind it had already occurred. Finally, we convinced him that his pessimistic anticipations would not come about, and he agreed to let us continue with the job. Wrong imaginations are dangerous if they are not demolished.

Imaginations and every high thing that exalts itself against the knowledge of God are to be brought into captivity to every thought of Christ. The high things are elevated barriers that keep us from receiving the Word of God.

Negative thoughts become hard to remove, once firmly ensconced behind the walls of your mind. Cast them down as soon as you recognize them. Jacob's first son, Reuben, delivered Joseph out of his brother's hands and prevented them from killing him, but if he had not tried to be a crowd follower, he could have prevented the incident. Some say it was within God's plans for Joseph to go to Egypt, and this was His way to get him there. I don't think God is so small that He couldn't have sent Joseph to Egypt another way. These young men were not walking with God; they were working for the devil, when they sold Joseph into slavery.

The conclusion was everything God had shown Joseph in the dream; the entire family had to bow down to him because of his position in the government of Egypt, second only to the Pharaoh. God was with him, and directed him during his entire life. This story of Joseph is a book within itself. Please read it.

CHAPTER VI

PHYSICAL EFFECTS OF UN-FORGIVENESS

Psalm 8:1 O LORD our Lord, how excellent is thy name in all the earth! who hast set thy glory above the heavens. Out of the mouth of babes and sucklings hast thou ordained strength because of thine enemies, that thou mightest still the enemy and the avenger. When I consider thy heavens, the work of thy fingers, the moon and the stars, which thou hast ordained; What is man, that thou art mindful of him? and the son of man, that thou visitest him? For thou hast made him a little lower than the angels, and hast crowned him with glory and honour. Thou madest him to have dominion over the works of thy hands; thou hast put all things under his feet: All sheep and oxen, yea, and the beasts of the field; The fowl of the air, and the fish of the sea, and whatsoever passeth through the paths of the seas. O LORD our Lord, how excellent is thy name in all the earth! KJV

It's amazing that the psalmist David saw the magnitude of the plan of God in making man. The Father God has created the earth with all its grandeur in such a way that humans haven't been able to duplicate. He placed the sun, moon, stars, and planets in their respective positions in the heavens. Each one uniquely contributes to Earth's providing comfort to its inhabitants. God operated in the capacity of a father. He instructed Adam to name the animals and then gave him the helpmate he needed, Eve.

Genesis 2:20-25 And Adam gave names to all cattle, and to the fowl of the air, and to every beast of the field; but for Adam there was not found an help meet for him. And the LORD God caused a deep sleep to fall upon Adam and he slept: and he took one of his ribs, and closed up the flesh instead thereof; And the rib, which the LORD God had taken from man, made he a woman, and brought her unto the man. And Adam said, This is now bone of my bones, and flesh of my flesh: she shall be called Woman, because she was taken out of Man. Therefore shall a man leave his father and his mother, and shall cleave unto his wife: and they shall be one flesh. And they were both naked, the man and his wife, and were not ashamed. KJV

Genesis 2:4-8 These are the generations of the heavens and of the earth when they were created, in the day that the LORD God made the earth and the heavens, And every plant of the field before it was in the earth, and every herb of the field before it grew: for the LORD God had not caused it to rain upon the earth, and there was not a man to till the ground. But there went up a mist from the earth, and watered the whole face of the ground. And the LORD God formed man of the dust of the ground, and breathed into his nostrils the breath of life; and man became a living soul. And the LORD God planted a garden eastward in Eden; and there he put the man whom he had formed. KJV

God breathed into man's nostrils the breath of life and man became a living soul. The word "soul" indicates a breathing creature. We all are breathing creatures, animals and humans, but we are not all made in the God class. Only man is made in the God class. This is shown to us in Psalm 8. the Hebrew word "angel" is the same word used for God, "Elohim." Therefore, when God breathed into Adam, the breath and the Spirit of God went into him and he became a living soul.

God and His new family, Adam and Eve, continued meeting in the cool of the morning to fellowship, the way He and Adam had before Eve. God loved this family so much that He gave them dominion over all His handiwork. The psalmist could not understand the depth of this love.

Then came the worst day of Adam's life, the consequences of which we inherited: physical and spiritual death. After man disobeyed God, he lost direct contact with his Father and became motivated by carnal reasoning and worldly intelligence, with a spirit subject to passions, desires, and assorted feelings that motivated him in new ungodly ways. Without a father, so many stumble onto the wrong path.

Adam now had the ability to direct his own efforts toward specific goals, dictated by his emotions. "Emotion" in the Latin means "to move." The terms associated with emotion are love, hate, fear, happiness, surprise, anger, determination, disgust, hot, cold, contempt. Emotions have a major effect on our lives, even the chemical balance of our bodies. Most of our actions dealing with relationship are based on our emotions. Another way to explain the word emotion; a person's reactions to things pleasant, unpleasant, appealing, repulsive.

In the case of Adam and Eve, they lost their dominion and home by disobeying their Father. God made provision for them through the blood of animals. But Adam lost his personal contact with the Father God when they walked in the coolness of the day.

The Healing and Peace of Forgiveness

I was told about two neighbors, friends for more than twenty years, who got into a heated argument which ended with them cursing each other out. They went their separate ways and would not reconcile.

After a few months, one neighbor gave in and asked his former friend to forgive him, but the apology was refused. A few months later the unforgiving neighbor fell ill and, within a year, died. This person's death surprised most of his friends because of his good health record. Holding onto anger, hatred, or un-forgiveness can actually lead to death.

When one doesn't forgive, it's like carrying around the person you didn't forgive. Let's say you get into a heated disagreement with someone and refuse to accept his request for forgiveness. You totally focus on the wrong done to you. Every time that person's name comes up, you get mad all over again. That 150 – pound person's weight controls your life, working on you mentally and spiritually, until you have spiritual and physical problems.

According to the Medical and Health Encyclopedia:

> Diseases thought to be caused, at least in part, by emotional factors are known as psychosomatic disorders. The term comes from the Greek "psyche", meaning spirit or soul, and "soma", meaning body, and refers to the effect of the mind on the body's health. In psychosomatic disorders, repeated emotional stress can cause dysfunction of structural damage in the body's tissues, organs, and organ systems by chronically stimulating the involuntary nervous system and the glands of internal secretion. This process is in contrast to disorders caused by bacterial or viral infections. A headache, for example, can stem from a common cold or from muscle tension caused by stress. The headache from a cold disappears when the infection is gone, but headaches from continual emotional stress may be self – perpetuated. Tightened muscles in

the neck, shoulders, and back increase a person's stress, which in turn increases tension in the muscles, which increases stress – setting up a vicious cycle. Chronic tension headaches often progress to chronic back pain, which can become disabling. The theory of psychosomatic disorders was proposed in 1950 and 1960 by Franz Alexander and his colleagues at the Chicago Institute for Psychoanalysis. They suggested that specific personality traits and specific conflict situations created particular psychosomatic disorders.

We can see how our emotions play a major part in producing various sicknesses. Anxiety, depression, repressed anger and fear are some of the negative emotions that may develop and lead to an argument. If we do not repent or control these negative emotions, they will cause us to become bitter. This bitterness may cause torment, preventing our body functions from operating properly.

Let's look at an example given by the <u>Illustrated Medical and Health Encyclopedia</u>, page 850, H S Stuttman Company, publishers:

A baby was born with a permanent closure of the esophagus or swallowing tube which passes from the mouth to the stomach. As a result, it became necessary to make an opening directly into the stomach through which the child could be fed. This opening also gave opportunity for the attending physicians to make observations of the effects of various foods, drugs and emotions on the action of the stomach. By the time the baby reached the age of 16 months, it had developed cordial relations with its doctor to the extent that his visits and observations did not cause any distress.

A technique was developed for studying the emotional reactions of the child. Another observer watched from a concealed opening into the baby's room and made a careful record of the reactions. Thus, standards were established for expression of contentment, joy, rage, depression, fear and other emotions. All such emotions had a definite effect on the child and on the reactions of the stomach. Incidentally, it was shown that a strange doctor could produce emotions quite different from those aroused by the good, friendly doctor. When the good, friendly, doctor injected histamine into the child's stomach, there was a copious flow of acid from the stomach wall; when a strange doctor tried the same test, the stomach did not respond with the flow of acid. The stomach wall normally pours out acid as an aid to digestion.

Emotions play a very important part in the physical condition of our bodies. When our food does not digest properly, it affects our health.

In a state of severe pain, fear, or anger, a person turns red because blood vessels on the surface of the body contract; the skin feels cold and clammy; the mouth gets dry because saliva stops flowing, and the tongue sticks to the roof of the mouth. The heart beats rapidly and sometimes so strongly that the pulsation can be seen in the blood vessels of the neck. These emotions also have an effect on blood sugar, which plays a critical part in body functions.

The encyclopedia shows also that blood pressure rises when a person becomes angry. When anger turns into bitterness and is held in a person's heart, it produces stress in the body. Doctors have learned that emotional and physical experiences of stress are normally caused by complex and tense situations.

The Holmes – Rahe Social Readjustment Rating Scale ranks a number of life events in the order of estimated stress levels. It ranks 43 critical stresses according to the severity of impact on an individual's life. The death of a spouse, for example, has a ranking of 100 stress points. Other stressful life events include divorce, 73; death of a close friend, 37.

Under stress, the body makes rapid physiological changes, called adaptive responses, to deal with threatening situations. In the first stage of stress (alarm), the body mobilizes its "fight or flight" defenses, to either resist the stress – causing factor or adapt to it. In this stage, the pituitary – adrenocortical system pours hormones into the bloodstream. The pulse quickens, the lungs take in more oxygen to fuel the muscles, blood sugar increases to supply added energy, digestion slows, and perspiration increases.

In the second stage of stress (resistance), the body begins to repair the incidental damage caused by the arousal in the alarm stage. If the stressful situation is resolved, the stress symptoms vanish. If the stressful situation continues, however, a third stage (exhaustion) sets in, and the body's adaptive energy runs out. This stage may continue until vital organs are affected, and then disease or even death can result.

In the case of high blood pressure, the pressure rises when the person becomes angry. People with high blood pressure are warned not to get angry or excited because a further rise in the blood pressure might result in hemorrhage into the brain and death.

The best way to reduce the effect negative emotions have on your life is to get rid of them. Stress experts frequently emphasize that stress can be good as well as bad, and advise their patients to make it work for them as a source of energy. They suggest the following ways to manage stress:

- ❖ Have a code of life and live positively
- ❖ Set priorities to avoid unnecessary time pressures
- ❖ Allow time for pleasurable activities such as taking walks or talking with friends
- ❖ Exercise regularly as an outlet for stress
- ❖ Eat a sensible diet to maintain the energy needed to cope with stress

Ephesians 4:26 Be ye angry, and sin not: let not the sun go down upon your wrath: KJV

The body experiences many different types of stress during a heated argument. No real damage is done to the body if anger is not allowed to remain over a long period of time. When a person hates as the result of an argument, the body is placed under continual stress. Remember, stress is the body's response to a threat or demand arising from a new or changing situation. The emotional and physical experiences of stress can be caused by a complex or tense situation. When a person holds bitterness resulting form an argument, stress builds causing destruction to the body.

Stress related disorders compose 50 – 80% of all illnesses, though stress may not be the only cause. Such disorders include high blood pressure, cardiovascular disease, arthritis and other inflammatory diseases, asthma, insomnia and other sleep disturbances, anorexia nervosa and other eating disorders. Stress is also related to migraine headaches, ulcers, respiratory or lung diseases, and skin disturbances.

Medical scientists divide behavior into two types, depending on an individual's reactions to stress. People with Type – A Behavior react to stress with aggressiveness, competitiveness, and self-imposed pressure to get things done. Type – A Behavior has been linked to increased rates of heart attack and other diseases. In the United States, two out of three men and one out of two women demonstrate

Type – A Behavior characteristics. People with Type – B Behavior may be equally serious in their intentions, but are more patient, easygoing, and relaxed. Life events may have a strong effect on an individual's susceptibility to disease. Stress is a major factor in diseases that have a significant psychosomatic component, that is, diseases whose physical symptoms are induced or aggravated by mental or emotional disturbances.

Some people in my own family have allowed the devil to turn them against other family members. Many of you go through similar situations. These type people always dwell on their negative experiences. We all have negative events happening, but it is how you deal with them that makes the difference. The terms associated with emotion are love, hate, fear, happiness, surprise, anger, disgust, determination, and contempt. Ongoing un-forgiveness leads to hatred, bitterness, anger, and unhappiness — negative emotions.

As individuals, we each have our own particular ways of handling stressful situations, as well as our own tolerance levels for what determines a stressful condition. People who allow negative emotions to motivate them and dominate their thoughts are always overly stressed. We should remember that negative feelings are the motivating factors that activate bitterness and cause a person to hate.

Ephesians 4:31-32 Let all bitterness, and wrath, and anger, and clamour, and evil speaking, be put away from you, with all malice: And be ye kind one to another, tenderhearted, forgiving one another, even as God for Christ's sake hath forgiven you. KJV

CHAPTER VII

CLEANSING AND HEALING POWER OF JESUS' BLOOD

Ephesians 1:5-10 Having predestinated us unto the adoption of children by Jesus Christ to himself, according to the good pleasure of his will, To the praise of the glory of his grace, wherein he hath made us accepted in the beloved. In whom we have redemption through his blood, the forgiveness of sins, according to the riches of his grace; Wherein he hath abounded toward us in all wisdom and prudence; Having made known unto us the mystery of his will, according to his good pleasure which he hath purposed in himself: That in the dispensation of the fulness of times he might gather together in one all things in Christ, both which are in heaven, and which are on earth; even in him: KJV

The moment a young wife discovers she is pregnant with her first child, her entire life changes. She transforms into a mother overnight. She informs her husband of the good news, and he likewise transforms into a father overnight. After rejoicing together for awhile, they call their parents, relatives and friends. Ladies start preparing for a baby shower. The conversation of the young couple changes from the daily routine news to the most important event of their lives, their future child. Strangers waiting in line at public places hear about the progress of the growing fetus.

The joyful parents begin planning which room will best suit the infant. The nursery must be near the master bedroom in case the baby wakes during the night. They design the layout and shop for furniture. Soon – to – be grandparents and friends eagerly help with the purchases. Everyone is excited.

The young couple begins thinking of the awesome responsibility God has given them — bringing another human being into this world. The mother ponders how to care for herself and the baby and make their surroundings comfortable. When the first movement occurs, she calls her husband and close relatives with the news. As the movements increase in frequency and strength, she makes more calls, never once thinking everyone may not want constant updates. She finds out the baby is a girl and imagines conversations they will have and all the questions her little one will ask about this new world she has entered. She thinks about raising her to love the Lord Jesus Christ and to walk with Him. Then the teenage years and the boys in her life. Oh, she concludes, as a Christian she will be easy to raise.

Now, let's look at the Father God first, and see if we can understand what He felt and His desire for the first child He was about to create. How excited do you think He was when forming the first man, Adam? He conceived the idea of having children, and went about designing a room in which they would live — a place filled with the sun, moon, stars, planets, seas, rivers, mountains, valleys, trees, flowers, fruit trees, animals and all sorts of wonderment. He recreated the earth for His child, making sure everything fit into its proper setting. This child would have all the comforts that could possibly exist in the world.

The time came to create this first child. God could have spoken him into existence, but this was extraordinary, a being formed in His own image and likeness. The birth of a new breed — not an animal, nor a tree — an immortal human being made in the God class, endowed with life everlasting.

I believe when the Father God readied to form man from the dust of the ground, He made an announcement and all the hosts of heaven gathered around to witness this awesome creation.

Genesis 2:7-9 And the LORD God formed man of the dust of the ground, and breathed into his nostrils the breath of life; and man became a living soul. And the LORD God planted a garden eastward in Eden; and there he put the man whom he had formed. And out of the ground made the LORD God to grow every tree that is pleasant to the sight, and good for food; the tree of life also in the midst of the garden, and the tree of knowledge of good and evil. KJV

Genesis 1:26-31 And God said, Let us make man in our image, after our likeness: and let them have dominion over the fish of the sea, and over the fowl of the air, and over the cattle, and over all the earth, and over every creeping thing that creepeth upon the earth. So God created man in his own image, in the image of God created he him; male and female created he them. And God blessed them, and God said unto them, Be fruitful, and multiply, and replenish the earth, and subdue it: and have dominion over the fish of the sea, and over the fowl of the air, and over every living thing that moveth upon the earth. And God said, Behold, I have given you every herb bearing seed, which is upon the face of all the earth, and every tree, in the which is the fruit of a tree yielding seed; to you it shall be for meat. And to every beast of the earth, and to every fowl of the air, and to every thing that creepeth upon the earth, wherein there is life, I have given every green herb for meat: and it was so. And God saw every thing that he had made, and, behold, it was very good. And the evening and the morning were the sixth day. KJV

The Father came down and met with Adam in the coolness of the day. This was their time together, and the Father used it to teach Adam, giving him His infinite wisdom about the history of the world before, Lucifer, the son of the morning, and his position in heaven and his downfall, and now his name was Satan. What a perfect example to demonstrate the results of disobedience. I believe the Father informed Adam of the existence of Satan, his fall and his habits.

Isaiah 14:12-17 How art thou fallen from heaven, O Lucifer, son of the morning! how art thou cut down to the ground, which didst weaken the nations! For thou hast said in thine heart, I will ascend into heaven, I will exalt my throne above the stars of God: I will sit also upon the mount of the congregation, in the sides of the north: I will ascend above the heights of the clouds; I will be like the most High. Yet thou shalt be brought down to hell, to the sides of the pit. They that see thee shall narrowly look upon thee, and consider thee, saying, Is this the man that made the earth to tremble, that did shake kingdoms; That made the world as a wilderness, and destroyed the cities thereof; that opened not the house of his prisoners? KJV

God the Father made Adam in the image and likeness of Himself and placed him in a special place called Eden, which means delight. Therefore, man lived in a "delightful place" with all power and authority over the entire earth and everything that was upon it. As the Father observed Adam over time, He decided Adam needed a helpmate. So He put Adam to sleep and made a woman for Adam whom he called Eve.

The real blessing came for them when the Father instructed them to replenish the earth with children. Think of the joy this couple experienced to learn they would have the creativity of God in them. They would make children for the Father God through their marriage relationship.

I think with all the joy and happiness surrounding the event, Satan's level of envy must have caused him heartburn, if it were possible. Here God had made children to rule the earth and replenish it with children like themselves. Satan understood that God had made this family of immortal beings to rule the earth, which included him. He knew that his power and influence over his demons would be in question if something wasn't done to stop Adam.

Satan went to work quickly looking for ways to maneuver the dominion of the earth from Adam. In the search, he found a willing helper, the serpent.

Genesis 3:1-6 Now the serpent was more subtil than any beast of the field which the LORD God had made. And he said unto the woman, Yea, hath God said, Ye shall not eat of every tree of the garden? And the woman said unto the serpent, We may eat of the fruit of the trees of the garden: But of the fruit of the tree which is in the midst of the garden, God hath said, Ye shall not eat of it, neither shall ye touch it, lest ye die. And the serpent said unto the woman, Ye shall not surely die: For God doth know that in the day ye eat thereof, then your eyes shall be opened, and ye shall be as gods, knowing good and evil. And when the woman saw that the tree was good for food, and that it was pleasant to the eyes, and a tree to be desired to make one wise, she took of the fruit thereof, and did eat, and gave also unto her husband with her; and he did eat. KJV

God the Father knew Satan's intentions, so He predestined mankind to be adopted into His family. He made man to live forever in a body, but through Adam's disobedience the curse of the sin nature came upon mankind. This appeared to be the end of God's original plan, which was Satan's plan. It seemed God's man was lost forever. This was Satan's hope. He didn't want the Father's desires to be fulfilled. God, knowing that man— a free will agent — could possibly fall, devised a failsafe plan for salvation. He would send a divine being to be born of a woman without the seed or sin nature of man. This Son of God would save mankind from his sin.

Since Satan was on earth, he knew of the birth but could not destroy the child. He was aware of the provisions but did not understand them or how they would be implemented.

Genesis 3:15 And I will put enmity between thee and the woman, and between thy seed and her seed; it shall bruise thy head, and thou shalt bruise his heel. KJV

Satan knew of a man coming to destroy his effectiveness over the earth. Therefore, from that day until Christ, he went after every male walking righteously before God starting with Cain and Abel. Now he really had a problem, and every righteous man born became his target. He must have become paranoid. After Herod heard of the Christ child's birth, Satan inspired him to kill every child under age two. I believe many habits of the un-regenerated man resemble Satan's habits. This is one reason we have to renew our minds to the Word of God to become God minded. Satan doesn't want you to become a child of God. God the Father made this entire earth for us to live on and dominate. We were made to rule the earth, and rule over the powers of the evil spirits living here. If Adam hadn't disobeyed God the Father, Satan and the evil spirits would have no power on earth.

But because of the actions of Adam, sin got a foothold on earth and in the heart of man.

Romans 5:12-14 Wherefore, as by one man sin entered into the world, and death by sin; and so death passed upon all men, for that all have sinned: For until the law sin was in the world: but sin is not imputed when there is no law. Nevertheless death reigned from Adam to Moses, even over them that had not sinned after the similitude of Adam's transgression, who is the figure of him that was to come. KJV

As you can see, sin entered into the world and was inherited by all men through the actions of Adam. This did not stop the love of God for His children: He set forth the second plan, giving us a chance to be reconciled back to Himself. This is where Jesus Christ came into the picture. In the Old Testament, God had made provisions through the blood of animals, as set forth in the law. Therefore, the law was God's covenant for His people. It taught the priests how the people were to worship, and live. When they sinned, they had to follow God's directions for atonement. To atone means to make amends for a wrongdoing or to cover over. In other words, the blood of the animals would be used to cover the sins of the people.

ATONEMENT BY THE BLOOD OF ANIMALS

Exodus 12:21-25 — Then Moses called for all the elders of Israel, and said unto them, Draw out and take you a lamb according to your families, and kill the passover. And ye shall take a bunch of hyssop, and dip it in the blood that is in the bason, and strike the lintel and the two side posts with the blood that is in the bason; and none of you shall go out at the door of his house until the morning. For the LORD will pass through to smite the Egyptians; and when he seeth the blood upon the lintel, and on the two side posts, the LORD will pass over the door, and will not suffer the destroyer to come in unto your houses to smite you. And ye shall observe this thing for an ordinance to thee and to thy sons for ever. And it shall come to pass, when ye be come to the land which the LORD will give you, according as he hath promised, that ye shall keep this service. KJV

It is recorded in history that about sixty years after the death of Joseph, a revolution in Egypt overthrew the old dynasty. Upper and lower Egypt united into one kingdom. Assuming the king formerly reigned in Thebes, it is probable that what Joseph did for Egypt as a foreigner and shepherd wasn't brought to the attention of the new ruler. Therefore, the new government wouldn't know anything about the history of the Israelites and their relationship to Egypt. The new government disliked and scorned the Israelites. Consequently, they were placed in the work force to build the treasure cities for the Pharaoh. When Pharaoh felt construction lagged, he placed taskmasters over them to get more work out of them. He made their lives miserable with hard bondage.

Hearing the cries of the people, the Lord Jehovah called Moses out of hiding and sent him to free the Israelites. The Lord informed Moses he would be to Pharaoh a god, and Aaron would be his prophet. You see, the Pharaohs were considered gods.

Moses and Aaron went to Pharaoh requesting permission for the children of Israel to leave Egypt to worship their God. Pharaoh said no, and to show he meant business, he made it even harder for the Israelites by increasing his labor demands upon them. The disadvantaged Israelites began wondering if God had really sent Moses to deliver them.

Many are like that today. If a project doesn't go without a hitch, they are quick to say God wasn't in it. When times get hard, faith is the order of the day. You have to know that you heard from God in order to move forward, when everyone is against you. We must not forget, the devils don't stand idly by while you follow God's instructions. Their job is to stop the work of God. Our job is to complete what He assigns to us.

Pharaoh forced God to bring plagues upon the Egyptians because of the hardness of his heart. God used the animals they worshiped as instruments for plagues, thereby destroying their faith in them. Their animal "gods" could not protect them nor control themselves. Moses' rod became a serpent and swallowed the serpents of Egyptian's magicians. The river turned to blood. Egypt was plagued with frogs, locusts, lice, and swarms of flies. Livestock perished, boils afflicted man and beast, hail and fire fell and darkness filled the land. (Read Exodus 7 - 12.)

In the midst of the plagues, Pharaoh became quite stubborn and the Lord Jehovah, the "I AM," stepped forward to show Himself mighty to Pharaoh, the Israelites, the Egyptians and the world. Pharaoh had demonstrated his power to withstand what Moses was bringing upon him during the first few plagues. The two human "gods" had met and the people saw their power. Pharaoh's magicians were able to perform some of the same acts that God had performed through Moses.

Now, Jehovah revealed Himself by hardening Pharaoh's heart. As he stubbornly refused to allow the Hebrews to be released, Jehovah pressed him with destruction unseen before in the world. When Aaron stretched out his rod and smote the dust of the earth, lice came upon man and beast. Pharaoh's magicians said unto him, this is the finger of God. (Exodus:17.) Although God instructed Moses to tell Pharaoh what would happen if he did not comply with His request, Pharaoh continued to harden his heart.

After the boils afflicted the people and the beasts, God hardened the heart of Pharaoh as the world watched to see who would win. Who was the greatest, the God of the Israelites or the Pharaoh?

God showed His absolute power over all things by destroying Egypt's way of life with the plagues. Then He prepared the last plague using the Death Angel.

Exodus 12:29-32 — And it came to pass, that at midnight the LORD smote all the firstborn in the land of Egypt, from the firstborn of Pharoah that sat on his throne unto the firstborn of the captive that was in the dungeon; and all the firstborn of cattle. And Pharaoh rose up in the night, he, and all his servants, and all the Egyptians; and there was a great cry in Egypt; for there was not a house where there was not one dead. And he called for Moses and Aaron by night, and said, Rise up, and get you forth from among my people, both ye and the children of Israel; and go, serve the LORD, as ye have said. Also take your flocks and your herds, as ye have said, and be gone; and bless me also. KJV

The Death Angel killed every firstborn in the land of Egypt. In the previous plagues, Pharaoh had servants to make sure he was comfortable. Pharaoh understood he was no match for the real God of Moses. Now, because of his pride, the firstborn of every household in the land of Egypt was dead, even of the cattle. He had no choice but to allow the Israelites to leave Egypt. He had met the real God and knew he was no match for Him.

Exodus 12:12-13 For I will pass through the land of Egypt this night, and will smite all the firstborn in the land of Egypt, both man and beast; and against all the gods of Egypt I will execute judgment: I am the LORD. And the blood shall be to you for a token upon the houses where ye are: and when I see the blood, I will pass over you, and the plague shall not be upon you to destroy you, when I smite the land of Egypt. KJV

The blood of the Passover lamb protected the Israelites from the Death Angel. From this period in time, God required the Israelites to use the blood of animals to atone themselves of their sins. This first Passover demonstrated the love of God for His people. He wanted to protect them and to be their God. One of the most important points God established here was the power He placed on the blood. He could have instructed the Death Angel not to kill any of the Israelites, but He used the blood of the lamb which would represent His Son Jesus Christ. The blood also protected the Egyptians who had accepted the ways of God. He showed us the awesome power of the blood of the lamb.

Leviticus 16:14-19 And he shall take of the blood of the bullock, and sprinkle it with his finger upon the mercy seat eastward; and before the mercy seat shall he sprinkle of the blood with his finger seven times. Then shall he kill the goat of the sin offering, that is for the people, and bring his blood within the vail, and do with that blood as he did with the blood of the bullock, and sprinkle it upon the mercy seat, and before the mercy seat: And he shall make an atonement for the holy place, because of the uncleanness of the children of Israel, and because of their transgressions in all their sins: and so shall he do for the tabernacle of the congregation, that remaineth among them in the midst of their uncleanness. And there shall be no man in the tabernacle of the congregation when he goeth in to make an atonement in the holy place, until he come out, and have made an atonement for himself, and for his household, and for all the congregation of Israel. And he shall go out unto the altar that is before the LORD, and make an atonement for it; and shall take of the blood of the bullock, and of the blood of the goat, and put it upon the horns of the altar round about. And he shall sprinkle of the blood upon it with his finger seven times, and cleanse it, and hallow it from the uncleanness of the children of Israel. KJV

OUR RECONCILATION

Hebrews 9:11-15 But Christ being come an high priest of good things to come, by a greater and more perfect tabernacle, not made with hands, that is to say, not of this building; Neither by the blood of goats and calves, but by his own blood he entered in once into the holy place, having obtained eternal redemption for us. For if the blood of bulls and of goats, and the ashes of an heifer sprinkling the unclean, sanctifieth to the purifying of the flesh: How much more shall the blood of Christ, who through the eternal Spirit offered himself without spot to God, purge your conscience from dead works to serve the living God? And for this cause he is the mediator of the new testament, that by means of death, for the redemption of the transgressions that were under the first testament, they which are called might receive the promise of eternal inheritance. KJV

The family, friends and relatives watch honor guards remove the flag from the casket and fold it with precision and care, as if not to damage the Stars and Stripes. Task complete, the highest ranking person takes the flag carefully in his hands, marches over to the next of kin with deep respect and reverence, and presents the flag. He takes one step backward, comes to attention, and salutes the flag very slowly, as if not to disturb the air surrounding his hand. As you watch, tears come into your eyes. It takes the minds of those present off the loss of their loved one for a few moments, seeing such honor paid to the fallen soldier. This soldier gave his life to help preserve the freedom of his country, or to help another people obtain freedom. During wartime, many such funerals go on around the world. We see in the media the pain and hurt on the faces of family, friends and relatives.

Soldiers fight for their country and many times their objectives aren't met. They can't guarantee a win when going out to battle. Our salvation is guaranteed to work through the blood of Jesus Christ. He didn't lose the battle over death and hell — He won.

2 Corinthians 5:17-18 Therefore if any man be in Christ, he is a new creature: old things are passed away; behold, all things are become new. And all things are of God, who hath reconciled us to himself by Jesus Christ, and hath given to us the ministry of reconciliation; KJV

Webster's New World College Dictionary states the word "reconcile" means to make friends again or win over to a friendly attitude, to settle a quarrel, difference, etc., bring into harmony.

Thayer's Greek – English Lexicon for the New Testament indicates that the word "reconcile" in II Corinthians, Chapter 5 above, means restoration or to restore to favor.

The position the human race was in, due to Adam's sin, could not be resolved by any other human being. There were righteous men who lived in such manner of holiness that they didn't see death in the natural form. But they didn't qualify to redeem mankind, because they all had the sin nature. Elijah was such a man that God took into the heavens without having seen death. God used him to kill 450 prophets of Baal, raise a widow woman's son from the dead, and predict three years of drought; but he was not able to be the Redeemer.

Therefore, God sent His Son Christ through a woman, to become the Redeemer.

Matthew 1:21-25 And she shall bring forth a son, and thou shalt call his name JESUS: for he shall save his people from their sins. Now all this was done, that it might be fulfilled which was spoken of the Lord by the prophet, saying, Behold, a virgin shall be with child, and shall bring forth a son, and they shall call his name Emmanuel, which being interpreted is, God with us. Then Joseph being raised from sleep did as the angel of the Lord had bidden him, and took unto him his wife: And knew her not till she had brought forth her firstborn son: and he called his name JESUS. KJV

The child's name shall be "Jesus for He shall save His people from their sins." Jesus means Jehoshus or Jehovah is salvation. Jesus came to save a special group of people and the 33 1/2 years He was on earth those people were His objective. Even though He came to the house of Israel, there were Gentiles who also submitted their requests to Him.

The book of John, Chapter 4, recorded how the entire city of Samaria received Jesus after He had a dialog with a Samaritan woman. She informed the elders of the town that she had spoken with the Messiah because "He will tell us all things."

Phillip went to Samaria after the death and resurrection of Christ and the entire town accepted his word. When the apostles, who were at Jerusalem, heard the Samaritans had received the word of God, they sent unto them Peter and John. They baptized them in the name of the Lord Jesus and prayed for them to receive the Holy Spirit.

Jesus called the Syrophenician woman a dog, and she persisted until she received healing for her child. Jesus stated, "according to your faith, be it to you." Although Jesus came to the Israelites, He did not overlook the person with faith.

John 1:12 But as many as received him, to them gave he power to become the sons of God, even to them that believe on his name: KJV

Those who received Jesus as the Christ received their requests. Today, we must believe on Him to be a member of the family of God. Jesus gave His blood to bring in the New Covenant. His death and resurrection represented the completion of the Old Covenant and bringing in the New Covenant. This reconciliation had to be consummated by blood.

Hebrews 9:14-22 How much more shall the blood of Christ, who through the eternal Spirit offered himself without spot to God, purge your conscience from dead works to serve the living God? And for this cause he is the mediator of the new testament, that by means of death, for the redemption of the transgressions that were under the first testament, they which are called might receive the promise of eternal inheritance. For where a testament is, there must also of necessity be the death of the testator. For a testament is of force after men are dead: otherwise it is of no strength at all while the testator liveth. Whereupon neither the first testament was dedicated without blood. For when Moses had spoken every precept to all the people according to the law, he took the blood of calves and of goats, with water, and scarlet wool, and hyssop, and sprinkled both the book, and all the people, Saying, This is the blood of the testament which God hath enjoined unto you. Moreover he sprinkled with blood both the tabernacle, and all the vessels of the ministry. And almost all things are by the law purged with blood; and without shedding of blood is no remission. KJV

Many of you will remember the incident in Genesis, Chapter 22, when God instructed Abraham to offer his only son to Him. In Verse 2, God told Abraham to "take now thy son, thine only son Isaac, whom thou lovest, and get thee into the land of Moriah; and offer him there for a burnt offering upon one of the mountains which I will tell thee of." Before Abraham could kill his son the angel of the Lord stopped him and showed him a ram. This act by Abraham, the father of many nations, allowed God to return the favor by offering His Son for our sin.

The divine debt had to be paid for the sin of Adam. Christ came as the second Adam. Now Christ is the mediator of the New Covenant and we enter into the Family through Him.

Romans 5:6-11 For when we were yet without strength, in due time Christ died for the ungodly. For scarcely for a righteous man will one die: yet peradventure for a good man some would even dare to die. But God commendeth his love toward us, in that, while we were yet sinners, Christ died for us. Much more then, being now justified by his blood, we shall be saved from wrath through him. For if, when we were enemies, we were reconciled to God by the death of his Son, much more, being reconciled, we shall be saved by his life. And not only so, but we also joy in God through our Lord Jesus Christ, by whom we have now received the atonement. KJV

It took the death of Christ, His blood, stripes on His body, etc., to reconcile us and free us from the wrath of the law. But it took His resurrection to bring us into the Family. The blood of Jesus redeemed the entire world, placing salvation at our fingertips. The worst part about the substitutionary work is that many will reject it. We are still like the first Adam. We have the will to reject or accept Christ.

Romans 3:21-25 But now the righteousness of God without the law is manifested, being witnessed by the law and the prophets; Even the righteousness of God which is by faith of

Jesus Christ unto all and upon all them that believe: for there is no difference: For all have sinned, and come short of the glory of God; Being justified freely by his grace through the redemption that is in Christ Jesus: Whom God hath set forth to be a propitiation through faith in his blood, to declare his righteousness for the remission of sins that are past, through the forbearance of God; KJV

We are leaving the curse of the law, which most people of old could not keep, and moving into an area where faith becomes the force governing our actions. It is now faith in Jesus Christ and the substitutionary work of Jesus. His substitutionary work involved the cross and punishment He took for us, which allows us to become Christians. We have a choice. God is so good that He lets each of us choose to join with Him or live with the devil, and go into the lake of fire with him at the end of this world. We all need to be redeemed from the sin nature and the power of Satan. We cannot obtain this through any method of our own. It has to come through Jesus Christ.

Romans 3:25 tells us that God has set forth Jesus to be a propitiation through faith in His blood, to declare His righteousness for the remission of sins that are past, through the forbearance of God. The word "propitiation" means to cause to become favorably inclined; win or regain the goodwill of, reconcile. The Father is constantly saying that He gave us favor, with Himself, to bring us back into the Family. His purpose to have children hasn't changed. He still has the same desire. We mustn't run from our chance to be a member of His Family. How can we reject the most powerful force in the world, divine love? In other words, Jesus reconciled us to the Father, by giving the blood needed to wash away our sins. The world doesn't have a sin problem. The world has a faith problem. People have faith in a lot of things, but their faith must be turned toward Jesus Christ.

Hebrews 9:11-19 But Christ being come an high priest of good things to come, by a greater and more perfect tabernacle, not made with hands, that is to say, not of this building; Neither by the blood of goats and calves, but by his own blood he entered in once into the holy place, having obtained eternal redemption for us. For if the blood of bulls and of goats, and the ashes of an heifer sprinkling the unclean, sanctifieth to the purifying of the flesh: How much more shall the blood of Christ, who through the eternal Spirit offered himself without spot to God, purge your conscience from dead works to serve the living God? And for this cause he is the mediator of the new testament, that by means of death, for the redemption of the transgressions that were under the first testament, they which are called might receive the promise of eternal inheritance. For where a testament is, there must also of necessity be the death of the testator. For a testament is of force after men are dead: otherwise it is of no strength at all while the testator liveth. Whereupon neither the first testament was dedicated without blood. For when Moses had spoken every precept to all the people according to the law, he took the blood of calves and of goats, with water, and scarlet wool, and hyssop, and sprinkled both the book, and all the people, KJV

Through Christ's act, He also became the High Priest. So we are priests unto Him for the people of the world. We are to bring them to Him.

Revelation 1:5-6 And from Jesus Christ, who is the faithful witness, and the first begotten of the dead, and the prince of the kings of the earth. Unto him that loved us, and washed us from our sins in his own blood, And hath made us kings and priests unto God and his Father; to him be glory and dominion for ever and ever. Amen. KJV

The proper translation of "kings and priests unto God" is "kingdom of priests unto God." Therefore, we need to take on the responsibility of the priests of God and minister to this unsaved world. Jesus Christ became the High Priest that gave what the high priest of the Old Testament could not. Jesus gave His blood for the sin of the world; the high priest of old could only use the blood of the goats and calves. But Jesus Christ, being the High Priest, went into the holy place not on earth, but in heaven once and for all and sprinkled His blood. The scripture said it was done through the eternal Spirit, it was an offering of Himself without spot to God. This provided for us forgiveness for our sins.

Colossians 1:14 In whom we have redemption through his blood, even the forgiveness of sins: KJV

Ephesians 1:7 In whom we have redemption through his blood, the forgiveness of sins, according to the riches of his grace; KJV

Acts 20:28 Take heed therefore unto yourselves, and to all the flock, over the which the Holy Ghost hath made you overseers, to feed the church of God, which he hath purchased with his own blood. KJV

The entire substitutionary work of Jesus Christ was done so mankind could be reconciled. He is the One Who planned this method: "to wit, that God was in Christ reconciling the world unto Himself, not imputing their trespasses unto them, and hath committed unto us the word of reconciliation." (II Corinthians 5:19) There is always time to repent of sin and ask God to forgive you, as long as there is breath in your body. When we see the effort God the Father went through to forgive us and reconcile us back to Himself, can you see why He will not tolerate our walking in un – forgiveness?

FORGIVE YOURSELF

Hebrews 9:14 How much more shall the blood of Christ, who through the eternal Spirit offered himself without spot to God, purge your conscience from dead works to serve the living God? KJV

The Father will purge your conscience from dead works to serve the living God.

While on a three – year military tour of duty in Germany, my family and I visited many small towns, castles, country sides and tourist areas. We had a wonderful time for approximately one year, until I was promoted and given more responsibilities.

During that time I was invited to practice with a band. After being asked to join the band, I returned home and told my wife.

A fanatic about music, I had put playing my alto saxophone before anything or anyone. My wife had known before marriage my devotion to music. Six months after I joined the band, the leader had some problems with the money and the members voted him out. He used our money to pay bills for his family. I understood his position as a young married soldier in Germany. The military didn't pay for his wife to come there and it was hard for them. My vote was to let him keep the money and just leave us. As a result, I became the leader of the band.

We reorganized and hired some new musicians. After practicing for a few weeks, we were booked every weekend and some week days. I no longer spent time with my wife and children. It never occurred to me that I was doing anything wrong.

My actions were very self-centered. I didn't have enough knowledge about relationships to understand what was happening to my family. Barbara and I have been married now for more than 48 years, but that 1 ½ years in Germany will always be a sore spot in my life. I didn't recall those days until I started fasting, studying the Bible, and praying. The past issues which had not been resolved between me and the Lord came to the forefront.

First, I repented to God and asked my family to forgive me. Although those things were repented of, often during my time of prayer and fasting these incidents and others came to mind and I actually broke down and cried, regretting not being the proper husband or a better father. It took the Lord to show me those years were gone, and there was nothing I could do to restore them. Now, I had to let my past be a lesson to be used to help others. I've lived this entire book, and know what it takes to forgive others and what it took to forgive myself. I learned never to compare myself with other people, to use the Word of God as my only guideline.

We had two children going to Germany and three when we returned: Valerie, Samuel Michael and Vaughn. Our last child Anita was born about a year after we got back, while stationed at Fort Lee, Virginia.

Forgiving oneself is a real problem, not talked about much except in the psychiatrist's office. The mind won't let go of things that negatively impact our lives, and we each respond differently. What affects one person may not affect another the same way. I'm sure I've done things that adversely affected my wife more than our experience in Germany. Barbara said to me, "Well, we weren't Christians." But many Christians have similar problems, or worse. Demons are here to exploit whosoever they can.

It was a long time after I became a Christian that God began to fine – tune my life. The real test of a Christian comes when the Spirit of God reveals things you can't believe are of your character. This started during my fasting period. Sometimes I asked Him to show me the real me. I wanted to clean my temple for the indwelling Holy Spirit. Forgiving others is also a problem for everyone but, personally, I think we have more trouble forgiving ourselves. This is especially true when someone else is severely harmed. We endlessly rehash the incident, searching for what we could have done differently to change the outcome. When we find a key to the puzzle, we say, "You know, if I'd done this, that never would have happened."

Many people have a serious problem with turning loose of bad memories. Friends and relatives usually drop reminders of the incident. Most people will begin to dislike you, regardless if you hurt them, someone they know, or someone they only heard that you harmed.

Depression often snowballs into a major concern for people who don't forgive themselves. A depressed individual can become emotionally unstable or suicidal. In their mind, they are unloved and not worthy of living. A suicidal person needs continual assurance they are loved and valuable. They must be nurtured back to mental and spiritual health.

Spiritually, they can't see how the Lord can love them because they let Him down and don't feel worthy of the blood of Jesus. They don't understand Jesus still loves them, and wants them to repent so He can help them through these hard times.

Physically, the first sign of trouble is lack of personal hygiene. They may begin to lose interest in cleanliness, fixing their hair, and dressing up. Some start punishing their body through various methods: self–inflicted cuts or burns, for example. By punishing themselves, they feel God is being satisfied. These areas of depression will contribute to physical illness if not stopped.

Bill and I were co-workers, but not personal friends. One weekend he went to a party and consumed too much alcohol. As most intoxicated people, Bill didn't realize his physical and mental faculties were adversely affected. On the way home, Bill had an automobile accident. A person was killed. Police cited him for driving while intoxicated and for causing the accident.

Bill was not a "bad person." He worked daily, went to church most Sundays, loved and cared for his family, and was liked by people he worked with. An average American, you might say. The case went to court; Bill was convicted and sentenced to jail for a few years. Most people considered his case closed. Not so. It ended for the courts, the next of kin, and Bill's family, but for him the guilt had just begun.

Satan reminded Bill daily that he had killed a person and destroyed two families. Depression became his greatest enemy. As a Christian, he mistakenly saw this as God punishing him for going to the party and drinking. He had to forgive himself.

Bill repented and had to work to free himself from guilt. We Christians must remember, the blood of Jesus is there to purge our conscience from dead works so we can do the will of God.

Consciousness is the state of being conscious; awareness; the thought and feelings, collectively, of an individual or of an aggregate of people. The definition itself shows why we have problems forgiving ourselves after harming someone else.

FORGIVING OTHERS

1 John 1:9-2:2 If we confess our sins, he is faithful and just to forgive us our sins, and to cleanse us from all unrighteousness. If we say that we have not sinned, we make him a liar, and his word is not in us. My little children, these things write I unto you, that ye sin not. And if any man sin, we have an advocate with the Father, Jesus Christ the righteous: And he is the propitiation for our sins: and not for ours only, but also for the sins of the whole world. KJV

I want to point out here that forgiveness is a very simple process. We ask and He forgives. He said to ask or confess our sins, and He is faithful and just to forgive us our sins and to clean us from all unrighteousness. To put it another way, God will listen, forgive, and then place us back into right standing with Himself.

How are we supposed to forgive those who sin against us? God set principles for us to follow: be faithful to forgive and let the person know they are placed back into right standing with us. This is the way resentment leaves. Now there might be a little hurt left for a while, but the resentment will be gone. This is why you must forgive, even if the other person doesn't ask you to forgive them. You must remove resentment out of your spirit before it can leave your mind.

Another point we must understand before going further: God paid for our sins through His Son Jesus Christ. Jesus' blood was enough to pay the price for the sins of all humanity. As children of God, we are to be like our Father, developing the same forgiving spirit. We are to copy the things He has done through Jesus Christ, and the instructions He has given us through the Bible. Remember also, forgiveness is a spiritual force that brings blessings to us from the Kingdom of God.

Forgiveness seems hard because we have been under the influence of Satan and the teaching of the world. King David sinned by counting the people of Israel. God had specifically told him not to number the people. God approached him about the sin and informed him he would be punished. Then He asked David if he wanted the punishment to come through the people or from Him directly. David said, "Lord, I put myself under your punishment because the people have no mercy."

2 Samuel 24:14 And David said unto Gad, I am in a great strait: let us fall now into the hand of the LORD; for his mercies are great: and let me not fall into the hand of man. KJV

Remember, we have said forgiveness is the turning loose of resentment against another person. God forgave David, but the punishment was not removed. Many have the wrong conception of God's righteousness. They view forgiveness as pardon. Pardon means to release a person from further punishment for a crime, to cancel or not exact penalty for an offense. There are sins which God will not allow to go unpunished. Now, don't misunderstand me and think every time something happens to you, it must be because of sin. Remember, the devil is still in this world and his job is to cause problems for Christians.

As I stated earlier, if you hold hatred in your heart against a person, it's like carrying that person around on your back all day and night, until the burden takes control of your life. You have to let go. In the military we went on forced ten – mile marches carrying approximately 25 – 50 pounds on our back. Soldiers who were not in good physical condition suffered. If 50 pounds can cause a person in good shape to struggle, what will happen spiritually and mentally when lugging around an extra 150 – 200 weight?

We can see hatred manifested throughout the world as wars escalate on every continent. We also see hatred and hardness in our young people as well as world leaders. Many leaders are not concerned with the welfare of the people they were elected to protect. Candidates portray themselves as honest and upright but, once in office, they lose their perspective. They find it takes a lot of spiritual strength to reject political corruption. Most of us over fifty can't believe what's happening to this generation. A few months after each election, citizens feel raped of their honor and trust, when seeing their elected officials beginning to follow the dictates of lobbyist groups. We live in a mad world where people are motivated to do evil by Satan, the ruler of this worldly system.

2 Corinthians 4:4 In whom the god of this world hath blinded the minds of them which believe not, lest the light of the glorious gospel of Christ, who is the image of God, should shine unto them. KJV

Ephesians 2:1-9 And you hath he quickened, who were dead in trespasses and sins; Wherein in time past ye walked according to the course of this world, according to the prince of the power of the air, the spirit that now worketh in the children of disobedience: Among whom also we all had our conversation in times past in the lusts of our flesh, fulfilling the desires of the flesh and of the mind; and were by nature the children of wrath, even as others. But God, who is rich in mercy, for his great love wherewith he loved us, Even when we were dead in sins, hath quickened us together with Christ, (by grace ye are saved;) And hath raised us up together, and made us sit together in heavenly places in Christ Jesus: That in the ages to come he might shew the exceeding riches of his grace in his kindness toward us through Christ Jesus. For by grace are ye saved through faith; and that not of yourselves: it is the gift of God: Not of works, lest any man should boast. KJV

We can prevent repeated injury from hurtful people by regarding them for what they are and getting out of their way if possible. Some of you may live with people determined to treat you wrong. They are so bound by the enemy that they are powerless in their efforts to resist him.

Living with someone offending or hurting you is hard. Anyone enduring such a situation should pray to make sure that staying is the right thing to do. Is it really God's will for your life? In other words, you may need to get out of the situation. This is something you might have to decide through prayer and some type of consultation. Life – threatening conditions call for leaving now and praying later for God's direction. Some love their spouses so much they deceive themselves into thinking the abuser will change.

I personally counseled a wife with that idea. Her husband was on narcotics, nonviolent at first, always short of money. He used all the family funds for his drug habit. The wife spoke with him about his problem and he promised to get help. He went for treatment but never stopped doing drugs. She couldn't get him to counsel with my wife and me. Eventually, she moved out of the house, purchased furniture and put her finances back in order. In a few months he began visiting her apartment, begging her to come back home. When she sought my advice, I suggested she wait at least six months to make sure he was drug free. She moved back with him the next month. Like I said, we deceive ourselves because we want our loved ones to change.

Before the year ended she reported he was now violent. I feared this might happen if he didn't accept the Lord Jesus Christ and get delivered. The violence occurred when she refused to give him money. So he started selling drugs to support his habit. She would have helped him more by not reuniting prematurely.

You may ask yourself two questions to determine your spiritual condition: Am I in hate or love? Am I joyful while praying for that person? If you aren't joyfully praying, you might be experiencing hate and need to repent. You may also need to consider your spiritual future. I personally know people living in similar strained conditions, and they aren't handling it well. They are angry at the world all the time. They have come to the place where they want their mate to die and go to hell. That, my brothers and sisters is sin. Some of you have reached this point and you need to get rid of the hatred and pain. Repent of this sin now.

Prayer: "Father God, please forgive me for the years of hatred I have allowed to fester inside me. I confess my wrong and will from this point on pray for (put the person's name here) salvation. (If the person is dead, ask God to forgive you.) Father, I thank You for forgiving me. I come before You in the name of my Lord and Savior Jesus Christ.
Amen."

Also pray these words with the psalmist:

Psalm 51:1-17 Have mercy upon me, O God, according to thy lovingkindness: according unto the multitude of thy tender mercies blot out my transgressions. Wash me throughly from mine iniquity, and cleanse me from my sin. For I acknowledge my transgressions: and my sin is ever before me. Against thee, thee only, have I sinned, and done this evil in thy sight: that thou mightest be justified when thou speakest, and be clear when thou judgest. Behold, I was shapen in iniquity; and in sin did my mother conceive me. Behold, thou desirest truth in the inward parts: and in the hidden part thou shalt make me to know wisdom. Purge me with hyssop, and I shall be clean: wash me, and I shall be whiter than snow. Make me to hear joy and gladness; that the bones which thou hast broken may rejoice. Hide thy face from my sins, and blot out all mine iniquities. Create in me a clean heart, O God; and renew a right spirit within me. Cast me not away from thy presence; and take not thy holy spirit from me. Restore unto me the joy of thy salvation; and uphold me with thy free spirit. Then will I teach transgressors thy ways; and sinners shall be converted unto thee. Deliver me from bloodguiltiness, O God, thou God of my salvation: and my tongue shall sing aloud of thy righteousness. O Lord, open thou my lips; and my mouth shall shew forth thy praise. For thou desirest not sacrifice; else would I give it: thou delightest not in burnt offering. The sacrifices of God are a broken spirit: a broken and a contrite heart, O God, thou wilt not despise. KJV

The Healing and Peace of Forgiveness

You should feel the anointing of God as it continues to wash away hurts and pains. Hatred will leave and you will feel the cleansing of the Holy Spirit. You see, if God anointed you to stay in that situation, there would be a knowing in your spirit that you are in the right place. Then, you would be able to stay in that position, pray, love the person and be full of joy. There would be a knowing that God has given you the mission and the victory. That person will change through your prayers and loving kindness.

Psalm 32:3-5 When I kept silence, my bones waxed old through my roaring all the day long. For day and night thy hand was heavy upon me: my moisture is turned into the drought of summer. Selah. I acknowledged my sin unto thee, and mine iniquity have I not hid. I said, I will confess my transgressions unto the LORD; and thou forgavest the iniquity of my sin. Selah. KJV

Here is a person refusing to repent, knowing silence was wrong. His bones were drying up, fluids blocked from them by un–forgiveness. Furthermore, the hand of God was heavy upon him day and night. God wanted him to repent. Un-forgiveness is a horrible thing. It will deplete you of life and allow sickness to overcome you. This is the reason we need to repent of our sins quickly.

Matthew 6:14-15 is so true. God will honor His Word. You forgive and He will forgive you. You repent and He will forgive you. It is always to our advantage to forgive.

CHAPTER VIII

HOUSECLEANING

John 16:13-15 Howbeit when he, the Spirit of truth, is come, he will guide you into all truth: for he shall not speak of himself; but whatsoever he shall hear, that shall he speak: and he will shew you things to come. He shall glorify me: for he shall receive of mine, and shall shew it unto you. All things that the Father hath are mine: therefore said I, that he shall take of mine, and shall shew it unto you. KJV

Let me tell you a true story about a little boy named Sam. When I think of Sam, the first stanza of the song "America the Beautiful" comes to mind. It goes like this:

>O beautiful for spacious skies,
>For amber waves of grain,
>For purple mountain majesties,
>Above the fruited plain!
>America! America!
>God shed His grace on thee,
>And crown thy good with brotherhood,
>From sea to shining sea!

Sam developed a godly love for nature and for his country as a young boy growing up in Edgecomb County, North Carolina. He was born in 1943 on "Shelton's Farm" between Speed and Hobgood, North Carolina. He doesn't remember his father ever being with the family. But his memories are filled with three people active in his life: his mother Mary, her brother Matthew, and a relative named Charlie Sherrod.

Sam didn't know if his mother had married, divorced or always been single. He never asked and she never said. He accepted the condition in which he found himself and lived his life to the fullest. He called Charlie, the oldest man in the house, "Daddy." In those days relatives often lived together and supported one another.

Most of Sam's relations lived on Shelton's Farm or farms in the surrounding area. They were sharecroppers, people who tilled the soil from sunup to sundown for a small weekly income and enough land for a small garden. At the end of the year after the crops were harvested and sold, the farm owners determined the profit and settled up with the workers. Normally, a sharecropper received just enough money to purchase basic essentials such as food and school clothes for their children, although some honest farm owners gave them a fair yearly settlement. From his five-year-old perspective, Sam didn't think his uncle or Charlie was ever satisfied with their share of the profit.

But Sam really enjoyed his boyhood. In the spring watching the fields being prepared for planting excited him. The men would normally disk the ground, plow it and rake or disk again to break up large clods of dirt before making the long straight rows. Sam liked the smell of freshly worked dirt and walking through it. Sometimes he looked out over the fields and saw birds eating seeds from the previous year's crop and worms dug up during the soil preparation. The rows were made to protect the seeds and later plants from being flooded during the rainy season.

Housecleaning

Sam's Uncle Matthew and Charlie sometimes let him drive the mules pulling the seeder, an exciting chore for him. Most of the young boys boasted about their chance to drive the mules or one of the farm trucks, which were used then for nearly everything. The mules were more gentler than the horse.

When the owner purchased his first tractor, Matthew was one of those selected to use it. On days when he left home without eating, Mary sent Sam to the fields with Matthew's breakfast. Even though Sam had eaten, those biscuits and fatback meat in that brown paper bag excited his sense of smell. There was something simply mouthwatering about hot food in a paper sack. Matthew rewarded Sam for bringing his food by allowing him to steer the tractor down the field when he ate.

Sam loved seeing blades from the seeds come through the ground. It was amazing how one grain of corn could produce a cornstalk which yielded two ears of corn with 600-1,000 grains on each ear. He observed animals being born and learned how their mothers cared for them, sometimes killing the weaker or sick ones at birth. Life on the farm intrigued him. His most enjoyable time was when the fruit ripened. He'd climb a fruit tree and eat his fill. He saw things firsthand that many only read about.

When his mother allowed, Sam went to his cousin's home to play or got up some kind of game with the farm owner's children. His mother and one of her cousins helped the owner's wife with the cooking and housework from time to time. Occasionally Mary brought leftovers home to share with the rest of the family, a real treat. Sam noticed those who helped the owner's wife were treated special.

During those years on the farm Sam never contemplated why his cousins had a mother and a father living in the same house and he didn't. Maybe it was because his Uncle Matthew and their relative Charlie were always around.

The Healing and Peace of Forgiveness

Of course, in those days, all adults cared for all the children. They fed them, corrected them, and if rain or other bad weather prevented them from returning home, they kept them overnight. Since Sam didn't like sleepovers, he always made it home before dark.

When the time came for Sam to start school, the principal allowed him to begin at age five because his birthday was in November. Sam, like many young black children those days, had to walk a mile or so to the school bus pick-up point. On freezing cold days when he arrived at the bus stop in front of a friend's home, they put his little hands and feet in a tub of warm water.

The school bus picked up the farmers' children at their front doors. This bus passed Sam and his cousins every day as they walked that mile down a secondary road. Why couldn't he and his cousins ride that bus to their bus stop? He wondered. Some days the traveling boys shouted derogatory names at him, although he usually didn't know what they said. One day he recognized the voices of the farmer's sons he played with and saw them pointing at him and calling him names. Needless to say, that terminated their friendship. Sam decided to never speak to or play with them again.

That was more than fifty years ago.

Many adolescents develop hatred toward peers who treated them horribly as children. Some enter adulthood hating entire races of people because of adverse incidents during childhood. Today Sam lives happily with his wife in Henderson, Nevada. He served seven years in the military, became a Christian and majored in engineering in college. Now he hosts several radio programs teaching the gospel of Christ. He acquired a Ph.D. in religious studies. He and his wife also teach nutrition.

During the summer of 1999, Sam and his wife visited his mother in Princeville, North Carolina. They went to lunch and did some shopping in Rocky Mount. While leaving one

Housecleaning

of the stores, Sam's mother stopped to speak with an elderly lady, who she later identified as the former farm owner's wife. Her husband had died some years ago and her oldest son now served in the military as Chairman of the Joint Chiefs of Staff.

When Mary mentioned her son's name, it caused an ungodly feeling to arise in Sam. He didn't realize the spiritual impact those feelings carried at that time. He didn't think it was hatred, but not far from it. His mother continued talking to them but Sam had stopped listening. He recalled that cold morning more than a half century ago when those farm owner's sons berated him. He learned that playmates or associates aren't necessarily your friends. He didn't say anything to his mother or his wife. He could see his mother beaming after talking with that lady. She thought so much of that family.

Sam also remembered a Saturday years before, when he went to North Carolina to visit his Uncle Matthew and Charlie. Sam found Charlie in the farm owner's yard helping him gather pecans. When Sam stopped to speak, his small children jumped out of the car and started picking up pecans and stuffing them in their pockets. The farm owner shouted at them to stop. Sam shouted back, telling them to get all they wanted, that his relatives had worked for those pecans. The farm owner asked Charlie who the "mouth" was and when he found out it was Sam, Mary's son, he gave the children permission to take the nuts.

Certain incidents affect people differently. Sam had considered the farm owner's son's cruel actions as a sign of rejection. Therefore, from then on he never got real close to many people because he feared being rejected. He set an invisible protective shield around himself and devised clever means of keeping people out of his "space," even his wife. Ultimately the Holy Spirit exposed the problem and provided a solution. God has a way of exposing our hidden hurts and pains to heal them.

Adolescent experiences contribute largely to the kind of relationships we will develop with the opposite sex and different races. It also affects a number of other areas, including our achievements in life.

As most of you know by now, I am that little boy named Sam. This one incident caused hatred to develop in my 5 ½-year-old heart could have destroyed my love for people and warped my entire personality. What happened to me would hardly register on a trauma scale, compared to the horrors too many children are forced to endure. The point of this story is to show you how little things can create big problems in the mind and heart of a child—problems that may remain buried deep within for years or even for a lifetime. My bad feelings about those boys lasted more than five decades. Every time I went to North Carolina and drove through the area, I couldn't help hearing their taunts echo through the fallow fields. I didn't think anything was wrong with me, but I had no love for that family. Being a minister, I knew what the Bible says about sin. I could have been deceived and not able to realize that my feelings were a sign of hatred hiding unrecognized in my heart.

The experience taught me to always be honest and fair with all people. During my seven years in the military, I think these principles were tested, and I never did anything to intentionally hurt anyone because of race, nationality or gender. I lived in accordance with those principles I established as a young boy.

Some years ago at a family reunion one of my cousins, who had polio, recalled our play times when the other kids would run off and leave him. He thanked me for always waiting for him and calling them back. I believe our relationship helped me develop personal character and sensitivity for the feelings of others.

While writing this chapter, the Holy Spirit asked me to search my heart for anything that might be hiding in it. This process brought the above story out of the depths of my soul so that I could be healed. We are offended daily, mostly by only minor offenses. However, this incident probably sowed the seeds for the way I think and view people today.

Once this hidden spirit of hate was revealed, I prayed and asked the Father God to forgive me for harboring un-forgiveness. I also prayed and stated that I forgave those boys. It was the boys I had hated, not the men they are today. During this process I could feel pressure actually lifting from my body. You may want to use this process before going farther.

Allow the Holy Spirit to minister to your hurts and pains.

BROKEN RELATIONSHIPS

Throughout life, we come into contact with people who have been nursing grudges and bitterness, and even walking in hatred for injustices inflicted upon them. These injustices range from very serious sexual abuse perpetrated by loved ones, marital infidelity, heartbreaking abandonment of a child or spouse, and incredibly painful divorce and custody battle, to a promise not kept or a cruel word spoken directly or behind one's back. The sad fact is we often rob, cheat, humiliate, betray, and lie to those closest to us.

Everywhere we turn there is pain, suffering and hatred: family members fighting and killing each other, children killing each other in our homes, schools and drive-by shootings, nations warring internally and externally, committing mass murder of their own people, and nations warring against nations, attempting to commit genocide on races or nationalities. Could some of these actions be the result of rage or hatred built up from childhood in the minds and hearts of national leaders? What causes one nation to war against another for no apparent reason? Why would one group of people want to annihilate another? What does it take to create such hatred in their hearts? Where does it start? I believe it started with Satan in the garden of Eden and he is still influencing people today.

I think we can trace most of these occurrences back to broken relationships. There is too much hurt and pain in our nation today. Broken relationships, among the most painful occurrences in our society, are not recognized as a problem by most medical associations. We see it between pastors and congregations, parents and their children, employers and employees, and among friends. I'd venture to say, nearly everybody has experienced at least one broken relationship. When a couple divorces, spiritual ripping of the flesh takes place that cannot be seen with the natural eye. The couple was joined together and became one flesh and one spirit when they repeated their marriage vows. The Bible shows us:

Genesis 2:23-24 And Adam said, This is now bone of my bones, and flesh of my flesh: she shall be called Woman, because she was taken out of Man. Therefore shall a man leave his father and his mother, and shall cleave unto his wife: and they shall be one flesh. KJV

Therefore, the breaking away or separation of husband and wife spiritually rips their flesh. Divorced people often become depressed. I once ministered to an ex-Army officer who was hospitalized for approximately six months after his wife divorced him. She left after he retired. There are many diverse reasons for divorce but the consequences are usually the same. Very few couples who call it quits remain friends. Most rush into another's arms, hoping to find a cure for the pain of rejection. Various degrees of rejection adversely effect every broken union. Some divorces have even resulted in murder.

In striving to overcome hurt and pain caused by broken relationships, we become masters of masking our feelings. It's hard for others to detect what we really think or feel. I did, and was still able to function very effectively in society. Consider our world leaders — do they respond to aggression from other nations or do they respond out of previous emotional hurts and pains? The media has reported that one of our presidents commanded attacks on other nations to take daily news agent's attention off their personal problems. How much truth do you think is in that report?

We must understand, adverse circumstances or incidents that occurred during adolescence can warp a person's character. Some of these problems that develop over a lifetime, if not repented of, may take more than a psychiatrist to heal. These situations often cause damage to the mind, destroying the means to rationalize logically and to choose the best method for handling sensitive situations.

Un-forgiveness prevents the Spirit of God from operating freely in us and hinders the flow of natural healing powers in our bodies. Our glands don't function properly when dominated by anger and hatred. On the other hand, walking obediently with God will bring peace and healing to the spirit, soul and body. Forgiving others is like watering flowers in the evening after a hot summer day and watching them perk up and look alive.

Matthew 6:14-15 For if ye forgive men their trespasses, your heavenly Father will also forgive you: But if ye forgive not men their trespasses, neither will your Father forgive your trespasses. KJV

We choose whether to forgive or not to forgive. However, the Father God specifically stated His actions toward those who decide not to. In my case, I didn't realize my situation, but once revealed, it was my responsibility to take the necessary action. It took this book to bring this incident to the forefront of my life. God's rules are cut and dry. For years we have been influenced by television and story books which usually present a Cinderella conclusion, regardless of the choices make. This is far from the truth. We must make the correct decisions in order to receive God's blessings. Yes, "God is good and His mercies endure forever." But when we break His rules continually, the penalty must be paid. God's mercies extend into the depth of our being to bring us into His grace. These are the fruits of the Father's love.

Jesus established new rules which superseded those set forth in the Old Testament. He turned the Old Testament standards of law into the Spiritual Law of Love in the New Testament. The Old Testament taught to inflict pain on our enemies. In Exodus, God gave laws to the children of Israel for dealing with their enemies and one another. His commandments are very specific and must be carried out as directed.

Exodus 21:22-27 If men strive, and hurt a woman with child, so that her fruit depart from her, and yet no mischief follow: he shall be surely punished, according as the woman's husband will lay upon him; and he shall pay as the judges determine. And if any mischief follow, then thou shalt give life for life, Eye for eye, tooth for tooth, hand for hand, foot for foot, Burning for burning, wound for wound, stripe for stripe. And if a man smite the eye of his servant, or the eye of his maid, that it perish; he shall let him go free for his eye's sake. And if he smite out his manservant's tooth, or his maidservant's tooth; he shall let him go free for his tooth's sake. KJV

God left no question about what He expected from His people. He was very concerned about rights of the individual. Improper treatment of one another is a shortcoming I find today in the governments of the world and even the clergy. If we understood God and His promises in this area, it would prompt us to walk righteously towards one another to avoid suffering the consequences of sin. In the Old Testament, children were taken to the city elders and stoned to death for disobeying their parents.

The conduct of God's people has always been very important to Him. He doesn't want us to have conflicts with our mates, family, friends or neighbors. Conflict causes separation. If a man and his wife have conflict, which is neither repented of nor amended, it will hinder their prayers and their function in society. We must learn to disagree without fighting over who it right.

The Old Testament taught an eye for an eye, and a tooth for a tooth, but Jesus came teaching the spiritual concept with a foundation of love. He set forth the spiritual law of love which totally changed the principles by which mankind must live. He stated that we should not hate our enemies, but to pray for them. It takes love and obedience to accomplish this task. This message requires the indwelling Spirit of God, self control and personal effort. Those who were personally taught by Jesus had to wait for the coming of the Holy Spirit to receive comfort and aid after He returned to the Father. Some disciples went fishing, and others went about reestablishing their old businesses; they did not have the Holy Spirit to confirm or help them understand the message Jesus taught.

Today, the Holy Spirit is living in us. He is our Advocate; the One called alongside to help us. Even with the Holy Spirit living in us, we must be willing to change, take control of ourselves. Without self control, a person can never completely change. When we change according to the Word of God, it improves our character. Godly character is developed out of our proper response to adversity.

SELF CONTROL

We train our dogs and cats to respond to commands but leave our children to train themselves. Our ungodly educational system teaches that children should vent their feelings, express themselves, do what they want; it ignores self control and accepting responsibility. Conversely, the Bible tells us to train a child in the way he is to go and when he grows older he will not depart from it. The Bible also tells us not to spare the rod and spoil the child. One reason the jails, prisons, and juvenile detention homes are filled with young people is because of ungodly teachings.

When we followed Biblical principles, the schools and streets were safer. Our children obtained better education from the school system and respected the elderly. These days most don't even respect their own parents. These same children grow up and become lawyers and judges. Once in a position of authority, they discard concepts that place control over their lives, such as the laws of God. They strive to remove God from the national judicial system, hoping this will satisfy their sinful consciences. At the same time, they try to use the judicial system to enforce decency in today's youth. They have sown ungodly seeds and now reap the harvest. The harvest is the incarceration of rebellious children. Unfortunately, many have parents with money who help them escape jails and prisons. But sooner or later their rebellious spirits come to light, and we end up with more hardened criminals stalking the streets like time bombs. The end result is mass murderers at our workplaces, homes, local schools, and other public places where people gather.

If we look at the original judicial system of the United States, we find it was set up in accordance with the laws outlined in the Old Testament. Over the past forty years, our legislators have been convinced by lobbyists to introduce bills that weaken the judicial system. Jesus stated that in the last days, the heart of man would become evil. We are seeing it in every area of our society. Today instead of our judicial system protecting the people of America, it aids the criminals. Lawyers work to find loopholes for their clients to escape punishment of the law.

Matthew 7:16-20 Ye shall know them by their fruits. Do men gather grapes of thorns, or figs of thistles? Even so every good tree bringeth forth good fruit; but a corrupt tree bringeth forth evil fruit. A good tree cannot bring forth evil fruit, neither can a corrupt tree bring forth good fruit. Every tree that bringeth not forth good fruit is hewn down, and cast into the fire. Wherefore by their fruits ye shall know them. KJV

It doesn't take much to see and evaluate the fruit of a person or a nation. At one time, the United States had evangelists taking the Word of God to all parts of the world. Now, people come from Africa and other nations to the United States to bring us the Word of God. We ministered to them at their time of need, and now they see that we are in need. Most of us don't see the need to be ministered to by people from other nations because we stand too close to the mirror. When a person dresses and inspects himself in the mirror, sometimes he's too close to view his entire body. We have to step back, turn on the lights, and set the mirrors correctly to provide more than one view. We need the front, both sides, and a means of observing the rear of the body. Without the 360 degree view, we have to depend on someone else to help us.

Nations formerly against the Word of God today are opening their doors and allowing evangelists to preach in their cities and towns. But the United States government and many of our national leaders are working to remove God from every aspect of the government and the media. The spiritually blind presently lead our nation. They don't remember world history and what happened to nations that rejected God and replaced Him with idols. ("Every tree that bringeth not forth good fruit is hewn down, and cast into the fire. Wherefore by their fruits ye shall know them.")

Hosea 4:6 My people are destroyed for lack of knowledge: because thou hast rejected knowledge, I will also reject thee, that thou shalt be no priest to me: seeing thou hast forgotten the law of thy God, I will also forget thy children. KJV

In short, people are destroyed due to ignorance of God's Word. They are killing, lying, swearing, stealing and committing adultery, as did the people of Hosea's day. We must remember that the curses of God for disobedience have not changed. God blamed the priests and teachers of Hosea's time for not instructing His people in His Word. I fear the same accusations apply to ministers today, as well.

Now we are taught to seek revenge. We're encouraged to sue if there is a slight chance of obtaining a large sum of money. Kill, if someone violates our rights or desires. Steal, if we want something someone else has that we can't afford to purchase. Lie, if it gets us out of trouble or into a desirable position. There are no morals and people don't understand moral principles. As ministers, we must teach the Word of God to bring people spiritual, mental and physical freedom. *Seeing thou hast forgotten the low of thy God, I will also forget thy children.* (A frightening thought.)

Christ was deeply concerned abut the welfare of others. He not only taught His disciples how to pray, but gave them principles that would bring blessings into their lives.

1 John 1:9-10 If we confess our sins, he is faithful and just to forgive us our sins, and to cleanse us from all unrighteousness. If we say that we have not sinned, we make him a liar, and his word is not in us. KJV

Christ is saying that there is only one way to get the Father to forgive us. So many times, we tell people to repent in accordance with I John 1:9-10, but we must go further. We must teach them to forgive others in order to acquire the blessings in these scriptures. Forgiving is a part of the confession process. We won't be forgiven by the Father God, until we forgive those who sin against us. This adds an additional step to the confession process. The word "confess" in this verse means to admit or declare the guilt of what we've done. This is a problem for some people; they are never wrong in their own eyes, and will never ask a person nor God's forgiveness. This is a major reason so many have not been forgiven for their sins and are reaping the consequences.

We must evaluate ourselves daily, to ensure we are walking upright before the Lord and our neighbors. If we're not getting along with one another, the question is are we really obeying the Word of God? We cannot effectively do the work of God or minister to others while angry with someone.

Matthew 5:23-24 Therefore if thou bring thy gift to the altar, and there rememberest that thy brother hath ought against thee; Leave there thy gift before the altar, and go thy way; first be reconciled to thy brother, and then come and offer thy gift. KJV

Forgiveness is one of the spiritual forces that allows us to receive answers to our prayers. You need to understand that the four gospels are really a part of the Old Testament. Christ came under the law of the Old Testament to fulfill the requirements of the law and the prophets. Therefore, when He spoke of a gift, it was a physical gift taken to the priest to be offered up for sin. Today, our prayers and praises are the gifts going up to the heavenly altar. If the problem with the brother/sister is not solved through forgiveness, God will not receive their gifts. We must be quick to forgive. Don't let anger take root in your life because it can turn into hatred and eat into your spirit as gangrene rots away flesh.

1 John 4:20 If a man say, I love God, and hateth his brother, he is a liar: for he that loveth not his brother whom he hath seen, how can he love God whom he hath not seen? KJV

CHAPTER IX

DEMOLISHING DEMONIC WALLS OF UN-FORGIVENESS

2 Corinthians 10:4-6 (For the weapons of our warfare are not carnal, but mighty through God to the pulling down of strong holds;) Casting down imaginations, and every high thing that exalteth itself against the knowledge of God, and bringing into captivity every thought to the obedience of Christ; And having in a readiness to revenge all disobedience, when your obedience is fulfilled. KJV

The spiritual force of forgiveness breaks down walls the devil has built in us over the years. It opens the door so God's blessings can flow into and through us, allowing us to minister more effectively to others. The spiritual force of un-forgiveness is from the realm of darkness. Like all of Satan's tools, it produces death and destruction. Satan uses very subtle methods to lure a person into un-forgiveness. Someone will begin telling lies on you or offending you in some way, and it continues until one day you get fed up. When Satan sees you in this state, the pressure is increased. His main goal is to get you into hatred or bitterness that could have been avoided if you had accepted the grace God provided to forgive the offense immediately. Know that the spiritual force of un-forgiveness is demonic and comes from the Kingdom of Darkness. This means the spirit behind un-forgiveness is evil. God the Father will not bless anyone practicing evil. Un-forgiveness is sin and God will not tolerate sin.

1 Samuel 25:23-28 And when Abigail saw David, she hasted, and lighted off the ass, and fell before David on her face, and bowed herself to the ground, And fell at his feet, and said, Upon me, my lord, upon me let this iniquity be: and let thine handmaid, I pray thee, speak in thine audience, and hear the words of thine handmaid. Let not my lord, I pray thee, regard this man of Belial, even Nabal: for as his name is, so is he; Nabal is his name, and folly is with him: but I thine handmaid saw not the young men of my lord, whom thou didst send. Now therefore, my lord, as the LORD liveth, and as thy soul liveth, seeing the LORD hath withholden thee from coming to shed blood, and from avenging thyself with thine own hand, now let thine enemies, and they that seek evil to my lord, be as Nabal. And now this blessing which thine handmaid hath brought unto my lord, let it even be given unto the young men that follow my lord. I pray thee, forgive the trespass of thine handmaid: for the LORD will certainly make my lord a sure house; because my lord fighteth the battles of the LORD, and evil hath not been found in thee all thy days. KJV

Nabal was a rich, evil, hardhearted man regarded as a man of Belial, which means worthless fellow, stupid: wicked or vile person (see Strong's Exhaustive Concordance under the Bible number 5037- Hebrew). His name fit him. Satan had used methods to build hatred in the heart of Nabal. Hate had blinded him to what David and his men had done for him. A person with a poisoned mind will disregard your good deeds done for them. I worked with a man like that once and found it difficult to do good for him. I had to do it by the power of the Holy Spirit.

David sent ten young men to Nabal to inquire for food. He instructed them to go in his name and tell Nabal that while his shepherds were grazing their flocks in Carmen, none of his servants were hurt, nor were any of his flocks missing. And in verse 8, they stated "ask thy young men, and they will show thee. Wherefore, let the young men find favor in thine eyes; for we come in a good day; give, I pray thee, whatsoever cometh in thine hand unto thy servants, and to thy son, David." Nabal stubbornly rejected the young men's request and sent them back to David without food or water. This antagonized David and his warriors. Now, David was on his way to destroy Nabal. The servants of Nabal told Abigail, Nabal's wife, and she went to meet David and his warriors to plead for mercy for her husband and her household.

Abigail asked David to forgive her. Here was a woman lining with a worthless fellow, doing everything she could to be a good wife. She had to go to David and humble herself before him and his men to save her husband's household.

1 Samuel 25:36-43 And Abigail came to Nabal; and, behold, he held a feast in his house, like the feast of a king; and Nabal's heart was merry within him, for he was very drunken: wherefore she told him nothing, less or more, until the morning light. But it came to pass in the morning, when the wine was gone out of Nabal, and his wife had told him these things, that his heart died within him, and he became as a stone. And it came to pass about ten days after, that the LORD smote Nabal, that he died. And when David heard that Nabal was dead, he said, Blessed be the LORD, that hath pleaded the cause of my reproach from the hand of Nabal, and hath kept his servant from evil: for the LORD hath returned the wickedness of Nabal upon his own head,

The Healing and Peace of Forgiveness

And David sent and communed with Abigail, to take her to him to wife. And when the servants of David were come to Abigail to Carmel, they spake unto her, saying, David sent us unto thee to take thee to him to wife. And she arose, and bowed herself on her face to the earth, and said, Behold, let thine handmaid be a servant to wash the feet of the servants of my lord. And Abigail hasted, and arose, and rode upon an ass, with five damsels of hers that went after her; and she went after the messengers of David, and became his wife. David also took Ahinoam of Jezreel; and they were also both of them his wives. KJV

Psalm 103:10-13 He hath not dealt with us after our sins; nor rewarded us according to our iniquities. For as the heaven is high above the earth, so great is his mercy toward them that fear him. As far as the east is from the west, so far hath he removed our transgressions from us. Like as a father pitieth his children, so the LORD pitieth them that fear him. KJV

The Father God waits for us to turn from our evil ways and come to Him. His forgiveness is always available. We will never be able to remove a person's transgression as far as the East is from the West, but we can remove it from our own hearts. I'm saying, don't let anyone get you into hatred. We categorize sin and establish our own definition of it and which sins are worse than others. This is not God's method. In His eyes a sin is a sin. Therefore, we must see un-forgiveness as sin.

When we change our view, it will be easier for us to forgive and ask for forgiveness. If a person curses, they are quick to repent. The same should happen if someone offends me or if I am made aware that I have offended others. Understanding the seriousness of holding the sin of un-forgiveness should motivate us to seek God's help in dealing with it. We have to do everything possible to break the stronghold of Satan on our lives.

2 Corinthians 10:4-6 (For the weapons of our warfare are not carnal, but mighty through God to the pulling down of strong holds;) Casting down imaginations, and every high thing that exalteth itself against the knowledge of God, and bringing into captivity every thought to the obedience of Christ; And having in a readiness to revenge all disobedience, when your obedience is fulfilled. KJV

Branches of un-forgiveness hide in some of us for years. Similar to the branches on a tree, these go out in all directions and are subject to many different consequences. The mind has the capacity to store information both productive and unproductive. We have to be filled enough with the Word and the Holy Spirit to understand the difference between the two. Unproductive information or events will bring forth unfruitful results and produce character flaws.

II Corinthians 10:4 indicates these unproductive events can develop into strongholds in our minds —walls, hard to break down. This is the reason some people will tell you, "No, I won't forgive this person." We have had people call us for help and, when the subject of forgiveness came into the conversation, they became very uncomfortable. Some have even started, "No, I will not forgive my mother or sister."

God doesn't want us to stay in un-forgiveness because He sees the consequences we will suffer, physically and spiritually. First, He wants us to repent and then forgive. He states we must cast down reasoning, judgments, decisions, or thoughts that are not in line with His Word. He even covers the high thing that exalts itself against the knowledge of God. Many times we allow our feelings to exalt themselves higher than the Word of God. Un-forgiveness can be one of those elevated things. Unfortunately, as we have noticed from this teaching, we are the ones who suffer the most when we refuse to forgive. God wants us to bring every thought into the obedience of Christ. That means to let the Word of God govern our thoughts. This is the only way we will have God's mind on every situation.

Don't misunderstand what I'm saying. It's not easy for us to put these things into operation in our lives. If so, there wouldn't be anyone walking in un-forgiveness and having to repent. Our problems come from years of incorrect teaching. As an Afro-American, I feel there are judgments, decisions, thoughts and actions taken daily that offend me. This has been the case most of my life. If I had responded negatively, I would have been killing, killed or incarcerated years ago. I had to learn to view my offenders through God's eyes and see them as He sees them. This was possible only after receiving Jesus as my Lord and Savior. I then felt sorry for those who could not understand God and His Family, made in His likeness and image. We all come from the same source and when we come against one another we are really coming against the Creator. I have learned to use this line of thought in my relationships, and it's helped me deal more effectively with sin in my life.

Philippians 4:8 Finally, brethren, whatsoever things are true, whatsoever things are honest, whatsoever things are just, whatsoever things are pure, whatsoever things are lovely, whatsoever things are of good report; if there be any virtue, and if there be any praise, think on these things. KJV

One reason some of us are in a fix today is because of inactivity, looking for the easy way out. In order to maximize our spiritual potential, we must practice Philippians 4:8. Yes, another area to relearn, but changing our thought processes will help us break down the walls of un-forgiveness. Practicing these principles will enable us to forgive and keep our heart and soul free of un-forgiveness.

Has anyone ever told you, "Don't get your hopes up"? They mean well, trying to protect us from disappointment. But, in essence, their statement becomes a hindrance. We need people inspiring us to reach for our dreams. We must encourage others to reach for the sky and not give up. Philippians 4:8 indicates our thought processes can change our attitude in every area of our lives. Whether aiming for higher levels in business, on the job, education, or in our spiritual life, these principles will help. If we really concentrate on using the principles outlined in Philippians, we will ask less for forgiveness and forgive more.

Forgiveness is one of the major keys to our success in life. We must learn to forgive those sinning against us and realize people have hang ups and differences that can eventually be changed through prayer. Many of them will be changed if we operate in love and not hate. As we set our heart on pleasing our Father God, the rest will come easier.

If you've been in un-forgiveness for years and feel there's no way out, there is. The most important part of being a Christian is understanding your blood didn't save you; the blood of Jesus Christ saved you. By grace He performed each step that allowed you to become a member of the Family of God. Your only responsibility is to accept Him as your Lord and Savior. The next step is to study the Word of God and strive to obey it. The Holy Spirit will help you do the rest. You may have trouble releasing someone who offended you. It hurt. . . destroyed your marriage. . . ruined a relationship with someone you loved. . . caused you to lose your job or business. Whatever, you have help. Pray and ask the Father God to forgive you. He will help you to forgive that person or persons.

One thing that happens when operating in un-forgiveness: holding grudges becomes easier. You must let all of them go.

Yes, there will be tears. But see them as stress releasers and let 'um rip. After prayer and forgiveness, you'll feel much better. Free of bondage that held you for so long. Walking in forgiveness will allow God's anointing and power to work within us mightily to minister the Word of God.

CHAPTER X

GOD'S PROVISION FOR FORGIVENESS

Genesis 1:26-28 And God said, Let us make man in our image, after our likeness: and let them have dominion over the fish of the sea, and over the fowl of the air, and over the cattle, and over all the earth, and over every creeping thing that creepeth upon the earth. So God created man in his own image, in the image of God created he him; male and female created he them. And God blessed them, and God said unto them, Be fruitful, and multiply, and replenish the earth, and subdue it: and have dominion over the fish of the sea, and over the fowl of the air, and over every living thing that moveth upon the earth. KJV

What a scene this must have been as the hosts of heavens observed the Creator God gathering clay and forming it into a shape made in His likeness and image. An image never before revealed in the physical. He completed His task and stood back as the hosts of heaven gasped, beholding the God man. Now the Creator turned back to the form and studied it. The heavenly host failed to grasp the magnitude of His purpose for man — to rule the earth.

Imagine with me: God the Creator stooping down, running His hand under the clay form, lifting it up to His mouth and breathing into the nostrils the breath of life. The hosts of heaven continue raptly observing the Creator. The outer surface of the clay becomes skin as the eyes, nose, mouth and lungs respond to the breath of God and begin to function. Man is alive. The Creator names him "Adam," which means ruddy. This man will father all the races of the earth.

What Adam saw while looking into the face of God is not recorded, but once again let me use my imagination. I think he saw the glory of God in brilliant light form radiating every color of the rainbow. The splendor enveloped him. Adam was clothed with the glory of God. The eyes of the Creator were like flames of fire, His feet like fine bronze, His voice like the sound of a soft wind. This was Adam's Father, the Almighty Creator.

What beauty Adam must have beheld in this home, the Garden of Eden. Colorful flowers in full bloom swaying from a soft breeze in warm sunlight. Limbs of fruit and nut trees weighed down with tasty offerings. Glistening fresh river waters and in the distance, sounds of waterfalls and the wind gently moving through the trees. Adam's heart filled with joy as he radiated the glory of God. He was the first man, a God man.

In the days that followed, God instructed Adam and, I believe, informed him about Satan and the dominion Adam had over the earth and everything that crept upon it: the fish of the sea, the fowls of the air, the sun, the moon, the stars, and the entire galaxy. Everything was placed in the trust of His son, Adam.

God the Father and Adam walked in the coolness of the day, establishing a father-son relationship. He spent hours instructing Adam about the universe, why it was created with the surrounding galaxy to keep the earth in its place and the moon and sun to provide time, light and heat. Adam had many questions and the Father provided the answers. Now it was time to name the animals. God said to label them according to their personality. Adam studied each one to find the right name. Meanwhile, God considered how He had created the animals as couples and said it was not good for Adam to be alone. Therefore, He decided to make him a helpmate. He put Adam to sleep and took one of his ribs and closed it up with flesh. Adam awoke and beheld this beautiful person God presented — Eve, the woman.

With God's purpose and plan now in motion, the heavenly host rejoiced to see the family He had created. God gave Adam and Eve their mission: to multiply and replenish, to subdue and take dominion over the earth. Their offspring would have the ability to feel, think, reason, come to sound conclusions and express love to one another and their Father God. They would be free immortal agents having the right to choose.

Genesis 2:16-25 And the LORD God commanded the man, saying, Of every tree of the garden thou mayest freely eat: But of the tree of the knowledge of good and evil, thou shalt not eat of it: for in the day that thou eatest thereof thou shalt surely die. And the LORD God said, It is not good that the man should be alone; I will make him an help meet for him. And out of the ground the LORD God formed every beast of the field, and every fowl of the air; and brought them unto Adam to see what he would call them: and whatsoever Adam called every living creature, that was the name thereof. And Adam gave names to all cattle, and to the fowl of the air, and to every beast of the field; but for Adam there was not found an help meet for him. And the LORD God caused a deep sleep to fall upon Adam and he slept: and he took one of his ribs, and closed up the flesh instead thereof; And the rib, which the LORD God had taken from man, made he a woman, and brought her unto the man. And Adam said, This is now bone of my bones, and flesh of my flesh: she shall be called Woman, because she was taken out of Man. Therefore shall a man leave his father and his mother, and shall cleave unto his wife: and they shall be one flesh. And they were both naked, the man and his wife, and were not ashamed. KJV

One day as Eve walked through the garden, a serpent began a dialog with her about one of the trees in the middle of the garden. I would think that he met her near the middle of the garden a few times before really talking about the fruit of the Tree of Knowledge. He could have started by telling her God was trying to keep something good from them. He informed her that God knew the fruit of this particular tree would made her wise, allow her to know good and evil. He pointed out the fruits were good for food and God knew she wouldn't die from eating it.

Eve fell for Satan's deception, for it was he who spoke through the body of the serpent. Once she had eaten the fruit, she offered it to Adam. No one will ever know what went through Adam's mind when he saw Eve with the fruit from the Tree of Knowledge. My first question to her would have been, why did you take that forbidden fruit? He made a decision and ate the fruit.

Genesis 3:6-12 And when the woman saw that the tree was good for food, and that it was pleasant to the eyes, and a tree to be desired to make one wise, she took of the fruit thereof, and did eat, and gave also unto her husband with her; and he did eat. And the eyes of them both were opened, and they knew that they were naked; and they sewed fig leaves together, and made themselves aprons. And they heard the voice of the LORD God walking in the garden in the cool of the day: and Adam and his wife hid themselves from the presence of the LORD God amongst the trees of the garden. And the LORD God called unto Adam, and said unto him, Where art thou? And he said, I heard thy voice in the garden, and I was afraid, because I was naked; and I hid myself. And he said, Who told thee that thou wast naked? Hast thou eaten of the tree, whereof I commanded thee that thou shouldest not eat? And the man said, The woman whom thou gavest to be with me, she gave me of the tree, and I did eat. KJV

Adam and Eve found themselves in a dangerous predicament. They had separated themselves from their only source of life. The glory of God withdrew from them and for the first time they discovered their nakedness. Satan's plan worked, he was able to persuade Eve to disobey God by eating the fruit. He used what the Bible calls "the most subtle beast of the field," the serpent.

I personally believe Eve ate fruit from the Tree of Knowledge for a few days before offering it to Adam. We are scientists by nature and I think she wanted to make sure the serpent was right before approaching Adam. Most of us will explore things until convinced we're right before publicizing our findings. She did not die immediately, nor did she notice any change in her life.

They did not understand the order of the family. Adam was given dominion over the universe, before Eve was made, in a covenant with God. In the beginning God gave Adam all power and dominion over the universe. After He made Eve and united the two of them as husband and wife, they became one with the power to rule the universe together. Therefore, nothing visible happened when Eve ate the fruit.

Satan knew he had to get Adam to disobey the command of God before he could take total ruler ship of the earth. Satan was interested in degrading God's most prized possession, the man. God had given total authority over the universe to Adam. Satan's next desire was to convince the man to worship him, instead of God. Satan wanted God's position. He stated, "I will ascend into heaven and exalt my throne above the stars of God, to sit upon the mount of the congregation in the sides of the north and be like the Most High.: (Isaiah 14:12-19)

Adam had to eat of the fruit from the Tree of Knowledge before any spiritual or physical change would take place in their lives. Even if the covenant was made between God and the two of them, Adam still had to eat the fruit before Satan could take complete authority over the earth. Remember, Satan is in charge of the earth now, but he does not have authority over a child or God. This is the reason the provision for forgiveness had to be given through Jesus Christ.

Once the glory of God departed, they saw their nakedness and the revelation of their sin was revealed.

The love and kindness of God moved Him to provide Adam and Eve with a sacrifice that would cover their sin. Adam and Eve's sin was an act of disobedience that rejected God as their Father. They didn't understand the magnitude of their act until later. There are two spiritual forces in the earth realm: God the Father and Satan the devil. The children's rejection of God as their Father allowed Satan to take leadership of their lives.

Romans 5:12-14 Wherefore, as by one man sin entered into the world, and death by sin; and so death passed upon all men, for that all have sinned: (For until the law sin was in the world: but sin is not imputed when there is no law. Nevertheless death reigned from Adam to Moses, even over them that had not sinned after the similitude of Adam's transgression, who is the figure of him that was to come. KJV)

As Romans 5:14 shows us, death reigned from Adam to Moses, even over them who had not sinned after the similitude of Adam's transgression. We inherit the sin nature because of Adam's disobedience.

God's Provision For Forgiveness

Genesis 3:14-19 And the LORD God said unto the serpent, Because thou hast done this, thou art cursed above all cattle, and above every beast of the field; upon thy belly shalt thou go, and dust shalt thou eat all the days of thy life: And I will put enmity between thee and the woman, and between thy seed and her seed; it shall bruise thy head, and thou shalt bruise his heel. Unto the woman he said, I will greatly multiply thy sorrow and thy conception; in sorrow thou shalt bring forth children; and thy desire shall be to thy husband, and he shall rule over thee. And unto Adam he said, Because thou hast hearkened unto the voice of thy wife, and hast eaten of the tree, of which I commanded thee, saying, Thou shalt not eat of it: cursed is the ground for thy sake; in sorrow shalt thou eat of it all the days of thy life; Thorns also and thistles shall it bring forth to thee; and thou shalt eat the herb of the field; In the sweat of thy face shalt thou eat bread, till thou return unto the ground; for out of it wast thou taken: for dust thou art, and unto dust shalt thou return. KJV

It appeared that God created the serpent to walk erect because his punishment was to crawl upon his belly in the dust. God put enmity between Satan and the woman's seed, Jesus. He also stated her seed would bruise his head and he would bruise his heel. Adam would work the ground which would produce thistles. God evicted them from the Garden of Eden, their home, into a hostile land. Adam experienced something no other man would ever experience. He went from immortal to mortal, from life to death.

God intended for man to live forever but his disobedience reduced him to a mortal being that would die and return to the ground. If you read Genesis, Chapter 2, you'll find that the Tree of Life was also in the middle of the garden. They could have eaten fruit from it, but didn't.

Genesis 3:20-24 And Adam called his wife's name Eve; because she was the mother of all living. Unto Adam also and to his wife did the LORD God make coats of skins, and clothed them. And the LORD God said, Behold, the man is become as one of us, to know good and evil: and now, lest he put forth his hand, and take also of the tree of life, and eat, and live for ever: Therefore the LORD God sent him forth from the garden of Eden, to till the ground from whence he was taken. So he drove out the man; and he placed at the east of the garden of Eden Cherubims, and a flaming sword which turned every way, to keep the way of the tree of life. KJV

Adam's sin caused the sin nature to come upon all mankind. God removed Adam and Eve from their place of comfort to a place of hardship and hard labor, a world in which everything would work against them. The land didn't work with them. The animals turned against them. The weather was uncomfortable. These afflictions came because of their disobedience. Now they had a new master, Satan.

Romans 5:12 Wherefore, as by one man sin entered into the world, and death by sin; and so death passed upon all men, for that all have sinned: KJV

Since Adam's fall, death has ruled over the earth. Mankind was now lost. Because of the righteousness and holy attributes of God, man's sin separated him from God. This was a law Satan knew very well because it judged him. I believe Satan contemplated that by getting Adam to sin it would force God to break His law and restore Adam. Therefore, He would also be forced to restore him (Satan) back from his fallen position. This way, He could over look Adam's sin. Isn't this the way some people think? We can tell how Satan thinks by the acts of sinful man. God could not and will not violate Himself.

Genesis 4:1-13 And Adam knew Eve his wife; and she conceived, and bare Cain, and said, I have gotten a man from the LORD. And she again bare his brother Abel. And Abel was a keeper of sheep, but Cain was a tiller of the ground. And in process of time it came to pass, that Cain brought of the fruit of the ground an offering unto the LORD. And Abel, he also brought of the firstlings of his flock and of the fat thereof. And the LORD had respect unto Abel and to his offering: But unto Cain and to his offering he had not respect. And Cain was very wroth, and his countenance fell. And the LORD said unto Cain, Why art thou wroth? and why is thy countenance fallen? If thou doest well, shalt thou not be accepted? and if thou doest not well, sin lieth at the door. And unto thee shall be his desire, and thou shalt rule over him. And Cain talked with Abel his brother: and it came to pass, when they were in the field, that Cain rose up against Abel his brother, and slew him. And the LORD said unto Cain, Where is Abel thy brother? And he said, I know not: Am I my brother's keeper? And he said, What hast thou done? the voice of thy brother's blood crieth unto me from the ground. And now art thou cursed from the earth, which hath opened her mouth to receive thy brother's blood from thy hand; When thou tillest the ground, it shall not henceforth yield unto thee her strength; a fugitive and a vagabond shalt thou be in the earth. And Cain said unto the LORD, My punishment is greater than I can bear. KJV

There is a big difference between the two offerings of Cain and Abel. One was the firstlings of the flock and of the fat thereof, and the other was an offering of the fruit of the ground. It appears Abel presented the best he had to God. Cain could have gone into the barn and picked up whatever

The Healing and Peace of Forgiveness

was at arm's reach. I don't believe their job titles had anything to do with God respecting one offering over the other. I believe the key is, "the firstlings" which mean "first fruits." Cain brought an offering in a religious sense, in his own "way." They both must have been taught by their father what was required to abide under God's mercy. I believe at some point Cain rejected his father's teaching and through rebellion the spirit of Satan took control of his life. Remember, what we see in the world today is not anything new. The devil has no new tricks.

Cain got very angry and his countenance fell. Who was Cain angry at? Himself because his offering was not accepted by the Lord? It doesn't appear that he had the right to be angry at anyone else. I believe he was angry at God. Look at the mercy of God at work. *"The Lord said unto Cain why art thou angry? Why art thou wroth? And why is thy countenance fallen?"* Now, we know God knew the answers to these questions. I believe God asked them to start Cain thinking about his actions and maybe provoke him to contemplate his motives. The scripture doesn't tell us how long this went on but it could have been for some time. In Verse 7, God stated, *"if thou doest will, shalt thou not be accepted?"* Most people would move to correct their mistakes, but Cain could not be reasoned with, not even by God.

Whatever the case, God says, if you do well, shall not your well doing be accepted? *"And if thou doest not well sin lieth at the door."* This phrase "sin lieth at the door" indicates a sin offering crouches at the tent door. In other words, God said to Cain, you can make a sin offering even if you didn't do your best. You can still make the correction by presenting a sin offering.

The same applies to us, when we recognize the opportunity to apologize and ask for forgiveness. "Let me make up for the wrong I did you. Let me take you to dinner tonight. I want to make up for my sin against you." God says there are still provisions for forgiveness. Many times we don't see the magnitude of Cain's actions. Nor do we see the love of God as He gave Cain a way to escape from sin. If God emphasized loving, kindness and mercy in the Old Testament days, we must understand that the New Testament provides something just as good or better.

In Verse 7, He states, *"and unto thee shall be his desire, and thou shalt rule over him."* What is he talking about? God is telling Cain, you're given a chance here to get your sin atoned for or covered. If you don't change now, Satan's desires will be fulfilled and he will rule your life from this point until you die. When sin gets into your heart, it takes dominion of your life. Look in James, Chapter 1.

James 1:13-17 Let no man say when he is tempted, I am tempted of God: for God cannot be tempted with evil, neither tempteth he any man: But every man is tempted, when he is drawn away of his own lust, and enticed. Then when lust hath conceived, it bringeth forth sin: and sin, when it is finished, bringeth forth death. Do not err, my beloved brethren. Every good gift and every perfect gift is from above, and cometh down from the Father of lights, with whom is no variableness, neither shadow of turning. KJV

Although Satan was not known to the people of the Old Testament, he was present. His method of operation is to give you a thought and continue to work on you until that thought takes root. Once the thought takes root, it will produce sin. This is the reason Paul stated in II Corinthians 10:5 to cast down every thought and imagination that presents itself above the Word of God.

2 Corinthians 10:5-6 Casting down imaginations, and every high thing that exalteth itself against the knowledge of God, and bringing into captivity every thought to the obedience of

Christ; And having in a readiness to revenge all disobedience, when your obedience is fulfilled. KJV

We must cast down wrong thoughts and get rid of them, grab every thought that doesn't line up with the Word of God and throw it away. Evil thoughts come, as stated in James, to draw us into our own lust and entice us with our own desires. Cain gave in to Satan's thoughts which allowed sin to conquer him. The results are clear. He killed his brother.

GOD'S NEW PROVISION

Matthew 1:21-23 And she shall bring forth a son, and thou shalt call his name JESUS: for he shall save his people from their sins. Now all this was done, that it might be fulfilled which was spoken of the Lord by the prophet, saying, Behold, a virgin shall be with child, and shall bring forth a son, and they shall call his name Emmanuel, which being interpreted is, God with us. KJV

People lived an average age of 925 years as each generation became more sinful. God could not tolerate this vast sin, therefore, He destroyed the entire earth except for eight people. Moses and his family were used by God to establish the new generation. Food for thought: God couldn't find enough people who loved and obeyed Him that could turn the heart of the world's population toward Him. Inhabitants of the world had become so evil God didn't see any chance of saving the millions living at that time. He brought forth the flood and destroyed every living thing upon the earth.

How long would it take to reach that point again in history? God selected men throughout the earth who had obeyed and worshiped Him to carry His Word. Still, there were 400 years of silence before the birth of Christ. The four centuries between the end of Old Testament history and the beginning of New Testament history make up what's known as the intertestamental period, sometimes called "the four hundred silent years" because of the gap in the biblical record and the silencing of the prophetic voice. After 400 years Christ was born and Light came into the world to save mankind from sin.

John 3:16-18 For God so loved the world, that he gave his only begotten Son, that whosoever believeth in him should not perish, but have everlasting life. For God sent not his Son into the world to condemn the world; but that the world through him might be saved. He that believeth on him is not condemned: but he that believeth not is condemned already, because he hath not believed in the name of the only begotten Son of God. KJV

Man through Adam had inherited the sin nature of Satan, and there wasn't anyone free of it on earth who could qualify to be the Savior of mankind.

Hebrews 10:5-9 That is why Christ said as he came into the world, "O God, the blood of bulls and goats cannot satisfy you, so you have made ready this body of mine for me to lay as a sacrifice upon your altar. You were not satisfied with the animal sacrifices, slain and burnt before you as offerings for sin. Then I said, 'See, I have come to do your will, to lay down my life, just as the Scriptures said that I would.'" After Christ said this about not being satisfied with the various sacrifices and offerings required under the old system, he then added, "Here I am. I have come to give my life." He cancels the first system in favor of a far better one. TLB

God prepared the way for Christ to enter the world through a woman, the same door He established for a human being to enter the earth realm. There is no way a spirit can enter into this realm and perform without a body in which to dwell.

This child had to be born without the aid of man who carried the seed of Satan, the sin nature. The angel of the Lord contacted Mary, a virgin, and explained she had been chosen by God to bring the God Child into the world. She couldn't understand how this could be since she knew not a man. The angel informed her that the Holy Spirit would come and overshadow her.

When this happened, she conceived and brought forth the Christ Child. God's plan to provide love, mercy and grace to mankind had worked. It came through Jesus Christ, Who came to provide salvation for everyone. God continued to allow man the freedom to accept or reject His Son.

Ezekiel 36:26-28 A new heart also will I give you, and a new spirit will I put within you: and I will take away the stony heart out of your flesh, and I will give you an heart of flesh. And I will put my spirit within you, and cause you to walk in my statutes, and ye shall keep my judgments, and do them. And ye shall dwell in the land that I gave to your fathers; and ye shall be my people, and I will be your God. KJV

God gave Ezekiel the prophecy informing the world of a new spirit to come. Mankind was in a fallen state that had to be renewed. *"A new heart will I give to you and a new spirit will I put within you."* The "new heart" is the new nature. He removed the old nature and replaced it with a new nature and a new spirit. The new spirit was needed for the Holy Spirit to reside in the renewed man. The Holy Spirit lives in man's spirit.

The Holy Spirit enters man when he receives Jesus Christ as Lord and Savior. He won't reside in the old spirit still connected to Satan. God also replaced the old nature that could not accept the things of God. Romans 8 indicates the evil of the old nature — an enemy of God — cannot receive the things of God.

Romans 8:7 Because the carnal mind is enmity against God: for it is not subject to the law of God, neither indeed can be. KJV

God gave man a pliable nature that understands and desires the things of God. Man cannot be happy without making this spiritual transition. Ezekiel 36:27 makes it clear there are two spirits involved with the total makeup of man. The human spirit and the Holy Spirit.

The Holy Spirit helps us walk in His statutes and obey the Word of God. Many think the Holy Spirit only helps us speak in tongues, but that isn't so. The Holy Spirit comes into everyone who has accepted Jesus Christ as Lord and Savior. Then that person possesses the ability to obey the Word of God.

The provision of forgiveness still continues today. When we accept Jesus Christ as our Lord and Savior, we are forgiven. Most of us could think about a lot of things we did wrong before accepting Jesus, but once we accept Him, those things are gone. God has made provisions for our forgiveness through the blood of Jesus.

1 John 1:8-10 If we say that we have no sin, we deceive ourselves, and the truth is not in us. If we confess our sins, he is faithful and just to forgive us our sins, and to cleanse us from all unrighteousness. If we say that we have not sinned, we make him a liar, and his word is not in us. KJV

According to this scripture, if we confess our sins, God is just or faithful to forgive us. So, then someone sins against us and apologizes or asks for our forgiveness, we should follow God's example and forgive them. He cleanses us from all our unrighteousness just because we confess and repent of our sins.

THE BLESSING FOR FORGIVENESS

Matthew 6:9-15 After this manner therefore pray ye: Our Father which art in heaven, Hallowed be thy name. Thy kingdom come. Thy will be done in earth, as it is in heaven. Give us this day our daily bread. And forgive us our debts, as we forgive our debtors. And lead us not into temptation, but deliver us from evil: For thine is the kingdom, and the power, and the glory, for ever. Amen. For if ye forgive men their trespasses, your heavenly Father will also forgive you: But if ye forgive not men their trespasses, neither will your Father forgive your trespasses. KJV

Let's look at the blessings that come from forgiving others and even forgiving ourselves. The spiritual force of forgiveness is activated when we forgive someone. Matthew 6:8 is part of the Sermon on the Mount. As Jesus taught His disciples the principles of living, He made an important point about the Sadducees, the Scribes and Pharisees standing on the corner, giving long orations and prayers to be seen of men. Jesus admonished us not to imitate them because our Father in Heaven already knows our needs, even before we ask. Then He took us through the model prayer. *Our Father. . . and forgive us our debts. . . As we forgive our debtors. . .* We need to ask forgiveness for our sins before submitting our requests.

Jesus continues by teaching forgiveness. I believe He is trying to get our attention here. In Verses 14 and 15, He said, *"For if ye forgive men their trespasses, your heavenly Father will also forgive you: But if ye forgive not men their trespasses, neither will your Father forgive your trespasses."* Jesus laid down principles of forgiveness, directing man's operation eternally. Remember, forgiveness is part of the nature of God; and as members of His family, those same qualities should manifest in us.

Therefore, we must follow the example of the Father God and forgive as He forgives. We have the provisions in us given by the Holy Spirit. Forgiveness places us in another realm, in an area beyond Satan's reach.

Mark 11:22-26 And Jesus answering saith unto them, Have faith in God. For verily I say unto you, That whosoever shall say unto this mountain, Be thou removed, and be thou cast into the sea; and shall not doubt in his heart, but shall believe that those things which he saith shall come to pass; he shall have whatsoever he saith. Therefore I say unto you, What things soever ye desire, when ye pray, believe that ye receive them, and ye shall have them. And when ye stand praying, forgive, if ye have ought against any: that your Father also which is in heaven may forgive you your trespasses. But if ye do not forgive, neither will your Father which is in heaven forgive your trespasses. KJV

Jesus makes this declaration again: *"forgive those who wrong you, that your father which is in heaven may forgive you your trespasses."* I cannot emphasize enough that when we forgive others, we activate the spiritual force of forgiveness.

At this point, you might want to stop and examine your life. Why are you having problems? If you have a sickness or disease that will not heal, or financial problems that persist, you may want to look deep within your spirit to see if there is someone you need to forgive. The spiritual force of un-forgiveness, hatred, malice, or strife may be working in your life. The scriptures say God will not forgive you, if you're holding something against others. I don't think any of us want to be in that position. God wants us aware of the blessings that come when we forgive others.

1 John 2:1-2 My little children, these things write I unto you, that ye sin not. And if any man sin, we have an advocate with the Father, Jesus Christ the righteous: And he is the propitiation for our sins: and not for ours only, but also for the sins of the whole world. KJV

This verse is not referring to someone practicing sin but someone who falls into sin by accident. There are people who plan to sin, this is called practicing sin.

Proverbs 17:13-15 If you repay evil for good, a curse is upon your home. It is hard to stop a quarrel once it starts, so don't let it begin. The Lord despises those who say that bad is good and good is bad. TLB

None of us can afford to have evil living in our home. This fact should motivate us to forgive. One key to forgiveness God revealed to me that indicated if I had forgiven a person was by determining how I felt when something bad happened to them. If you're glad your neighbor had a car accident, you have the wrong spirit and have not forgiven them yet.

We also must be careful about the words we use about others because they can work against us as well. Verse 14 states, *"It is hard to stop a quarrel once it starts, so don't let it begin."* Repel contention, don't let it come near or become a part of you. Hate, malice and strife are forms of contention which we can't allow into our daily routine. To have a happy and prosperous home keep out strife and malice, and hatred will never develop.

We need to rejoice continually, even when things are not going our way. Although we must forgive, we should remember that we can't force anyone to forgive us or receive our forgiveness. A broken spirit dries the bones. A broken spirit comes from many things, but one in particular is strife. Strife will lead a person into hatred and animosity. Whatsoever we sow, we reap, so says the law of sowing and reaping or the law of reciprocity. Proverbs 17:14 above says *"If you repay evil for good, a curse is upon your home."*

Proverbs 17:22 A cheerful heart does good like medicine, but a broken spirit makes one sick. TLB

Nothing ruins health more that grief, continual worry, anxiety, fretfulness, bad temper, hatred, malice or bitterness. These troublemakers must be eradicated if we want good health and a life filled with joy. These are the physical things un-forgiveness will bring into our lives. We must forgive and continue to develop our relationship with the Father God. Family members go without speaking for years, not because they don't know the location of each other, but because they're mad at each other. We must walk in love and forgiveness in order to obtain the blessings of the Lord.

THE CURSES OF UN-FORGIVENESS

Matthew 18:21-35 Then came Peter to him, and said, Lord, how oft shall my brother sin against me, and I forgive him? till seven times? Jesus saith unto him, I say not unto thee, Until seven times: but, until seventy times seven. Therefore is the kingdom of heaven likened unto a certain king, which would take account of his servants. And when he had begun to reckon, one was brought unto him, which owed him ten thousand talents. But forasmuch as he had not to pay, his lord commanded him to be sold, and his wife, and children, and all that he had, and payment to be made. The servant therefore fell down, and worshipped him, saying, Lord, have patience with me, and I will pay thee all. Then the lord of that servant was moved with compassion, and loosed him, and forgave him the debt. But the same servant went out, and found one of his fellowservants, which owed him an hundred pence: and he laid hands on him, and took him by the throat, saying, Pay me that thou owest. And his fellowservant fell down at his feet, and besought him, saying, Have patience with me, and I will pay thee all. And he would not: but went and cast him into prison, till he should pay the debt. So when his fellowservants saw what was done, they were very sorry, and came and told unto their lord all that was done. Then his lord, after that he had called him, said unto him, O thou wicked servant, I forgave thee all that debt, because thou desiredst me: Shouldest not thou also have had compassion on thy fellowservant, even as I had pity on thee? And his lord was wroth, and delivered him to the tormentors, till he should pay all that was due unto him. So likewise shall my heavenly Father do also unto you, if ye from your hearts forgive not every one his brother their trespasses. KJV

The curses of un-forgiveness are great and the curses of un-repented sins are great. Notice the history of Israel: The Israelites had a terrible time when they disobeyed God. Led into idolatry by a king, they were cursed and taken into bondage and enslaved. After repenting and receiving God's forgiveness, they began to prosper. These same principles still apply to us today.

Wanting to know how often he should forgive his brother, Peter asked if seven times was enough. Jesus answered, *"I say unto you until seven times seventy."* Of course, seven times seventy is only a number given to demonstrate the importance of forgiveness. I believe Jesus is saying forgive your brother as many times as necessary, no matter the number. Don't keep count. Forgiveness is medicinal for you. Verse 23 above shows us this king had several servants overseeing particular projects. One servant misused the king's money and owed him ten thousand talents. On today's money market, ten thousand gold talents is more than $200 million; for silver talents, more than $19 million. So we see the servant owed the king a lot of money. The Bible doesn't state if the talents were gold or silver.

Verse 23 continues with Jesus comparing this king to the kingdom of heaven. He says the servant asked and the king forgave him what amounted to millions of dollars of indebtedness. In Verse 28 Jesus continues answering Peter's question with the parable. The servant found his fellow servant who owed him the equivalent of $17 and demanded payment. When asked for patience, he refused forgiveness and had him imprisoned until the debt was paid.

Many times we as Christians fall into this category. Jesus has gone away to the Father for awhile and left us in charge of our families or ministries. When He returns He will ask us for an accounting.

We can see what's wrong with others, but what about ourselves? We ask God to forgive us, but when someone asks us to forgive them, are we quick to forgive? Or do we want to punish them just a little bit? Yes, it is human to want to punish people but God says we must be like Him. Acting in such a manner, I feel good walking in love and ongoing forgiveness.

People can persuade us to hate others. For example, I witnessed a guy convince his fellow employees to turn en masse against a person he disliked and envied. His coworkers didn't understand the reasons but, because of his position in the group, they went along with him.

We must never follow such actions, but pray for people we dislike. We violate the Word of God by participating in hatred.

Again in Verses 19 and 30, the servant would not forgive a mere $17 debt, after he was forgiven millions of dollars of indebtedness — a typical example of the fallen nature of mankind. But it is the same with us; Jesus Christ has forgiven us and washed us with His Blood, yet we sometimes have problems forgiving one another. In Verse 31, we see people astonished when the servant who had been forgiven such a large debt threw his fellow servant in jail over so little.

People were full of sorrow and told the king. In Verse 32, the king called the servant wicked and said, *"O thou wicked servant, I forgave thee all that debt, because thou desiredst me: Shouldest not thou also have had compassion on thy fellowservant, even as I had pity on thee?"* The king called him wicked for not forgiving and showing compassion for his fellow servant. The king was angry and delivered him to the jailer until he could pay all that was due him. *"So likewise shall my heavenly Father do also unto you, if ye from your hearts forgive not every one his brother their trespasses."* Christ brings the parable back to us, saying God works the same way as this king.

If we don't forgive our brother and have compassion, God will not forgive us or have compassion upon us.

CLOSING STATEMENT

By
Barbara Walston

During more than 32 years of walking with the Lord, I have seen many people unhappy because they refuse to forgive their offenders. Blessed with love and compassion for my fellow man, it upsets me to witness this needless suffering, knowing the solution is so simple. What bothers me most is the eternal danger of harboring un-forgiveness.

What is the eternal fate of a person who leaves this life in bitterness after having experienced salvation and counted on spending eternity with the Lord? Have they deceived themselves into believing the Lord will overlook this shortcoming and take them into glory to live with Him forever?

Spending eternity in hell carries a far greater consequence than spending a lifetime in misery. Hell offers no second chance, no opportunity to turn back.

I pray this book has inspired and motivated you to forgive all who have offended you and, with the help of the Lord, to never hold un-forgiveness against anyone again.

CPSIA information can be obtained at www.ICGtesting.com
Printed in the USA
BVOW020133130712
295070BV00001B/6/P